The Official RED BOOK®
A GUIDE BOOK OF
MODERN UNITED STATES
PROOF COIN SETS

Silver and Clad Sets
1936 to Date

Written by
David W. Lange

Foreword by
Q. David Bowers

Valuations Editor
Lawrence Stack

Whitman Publishing, LLC
PUBLISHING SINCE 1934

Art Direction: Matthew W. Jeffirs
Book Design: Robert A. Cashatt and Jennifer L. Williams
Editors: Jennifer Corbett and Dennis Tucker
Publisher: Dennis Tucker

ISBN: 0-79481-764-5

Printed in Canada

The Official RED BOOK® Series includes:

- *A Guide Book of Morgan Silver Dollars*
- *A Guide Book of Double Eagle Gold Coins*
- *A Guide Book of United States Type Coins*
- *A Guide Book of Modern United States Proof Coin Sets*
- *A Guide Book of United States Nickel Five-Cent Pieces*
- *A Guide Book of Flying Eagle and Indian Cents*
- *A Guide Book of United States Commemorative Coins*
- *A Guide Book of United States Barber Silver Coins*
- *A Guide Book of United States Liberty Seated Silver Coins*

TABLE OF CONTENTS

A gallery of full-color images appears after page 192.

ABOUT THE AUTHOR

David W. Lange, Director of Research for NGC, is a professional numismatist and a prolific author. In addition to writing several books and hundreds of magazine articles on United States coinage, he has been a columnist for the American Numismatic Association's monthly journal, *Numismatist*, since 1988. He lives in Florida with his wife Alba and their daughter Amanda.

ACKNOWLEDGEMENTS

When it comes to knowing a series well, there are few people more expert than one who deals in that series on a daily basis. In the field of Proof sets, Rick Tomaska is just such an expert. He not only provided the pricing for certified Proof sets included in this book, but he also furnished valuable guidance in determining what material should be included.

Lawrence R. Stack also provided many prices. An experienced collector and a key figure in the firm of Stack's Rare Coins, he is a member of numerous numismatic guilds and associations, and a well-known writer and editor in the numismatic field.

Kenneth Bressett provided pricing for uncertified Proof sets. Well-known in the numismatic world, Bressett is the author of many works, a past president of the American Numismatic Association, and longtime editor of *A Guide Book of United States Coins* (popularly known as the Red Book).

Jennifer Corbett, Diana Plattner, and Dennis Tucker wrote the "Collector's Notebook" entries.

FOREWORD
BY Q. DAVID BOWERS

There is no doubt that Proof coins are *special*, today as well as they were years ago. Made from dies specially polished at the Mint, and carefully struck, such pieces were first intended for presentation to diplomats and other officials, as well as distribution to interested numismatists. As David W. Lange explains, beginning in 1858, they were widely sold to collectors, after which time Proofs have been made in several long runs, punctuated by gaps of no production.

The author treats Proof sets from 1936 to date, varieties once thought ordinary by collectors and often purchased in a casual manner just to keep current with new coinage. In recent years, that has changed, and Proofs of the 1936 to 1942 era have been studied for varieties and characteristics that are quite different from those of 1950 to 1964, and different still from those of today. Sometimes a small and scarcely noticeable die detail can mean a large difference in price (a good way for you to recoup the modest cost of this book if you identify something special!). The author, longtime numismatic guru and question-answerer for customers of the Numismatic Guaranty Corporation of America (NGC), and a fine help to me with research questions over a long period of years, taps his deep knowledge of modern Proofs—a very popular area of the market.

Distinctions that were either not recognized or not emphasized—such as doubled dies and deep cameo contrasts—are described in detail. Although I consider myself to be fairly conversant with modern Proof coinage, until reading this book, I did not know of the complexity involved! Now I know that even among sets of the past several decades, two adjacent dates can have widely different characteristics as to contrast, die sharpness, and more. The reader of this book will be at a distinct advantage in the marketplace, with information not generally available even piecemeal in popular texts, and nowhere available in a single place until now.

Beyond interesting varieties, David W. Lange takes the reader on a veritable behind-the-scenes view of grading, surface quality, market preferences, popularity, and more, again based upon his NGC experience, certainly a rare asset. Now, you will be able to study and appreciate the sets you already own and use special knowledge when you consider buying those you do not have.

I congratulate Dave Lange on creating a work that will be useful to all interested in this fascinating field. I know I will refer to my copy constantly.

Q. David Bowers
Wolfeboro, NH
March 2005

INTRODUCTION
BY DAVID W. LANGE

I bought my first Proof set in 1971. In fact, it was a 1971-S Proof set of five coins that I purchased for $5 exactly, and I have been on the United States Mint's mailing list ever since.

Though I had been a collector of coins from circulation for a few years by then, I was dazzled by the brilliance and perfection of these five beauties. The attractive plastic case certainly added to their appeal. It was like a coin collection in itself—no album required. Though I was not aware of it at the time, by 1971, the packaging was the evolutionary result of many years' development. In contrast, Proof sets of 1955 and earlier were packaged in small cardboard storage boxes and were pretty much do-it-yourself jobs as far as presentation was concerned.

From a local coin shop owner, I soon learned the great secret to shopping for Proof sets. Pssst! Look for the cameo! In 1971, most Proof sets were still issued with a fully brilliant finish on both fields and devices. Only the lucky few received coins struck from fresh dies that had white frosting on the raised portions of the design. Back then, these coins were sought by a handful of pioneers.

Still a teenager, I did not have the means to travel to coin shows to shop for Proof sets, so I just rolled the dice each autumn by ordering next year's set from the Old San Francisco Mint Museum. In a time long before the Internet, toll-free numbers, and other modern conveniences, mailing list customers such as myself received a rectangular data card with holes punched into it that would let the Mint's mainframe computer know who I was when it received my order. In addition to returning the card, I had to remove a series of tabs from another card that corresponded to the number of sets I was purchasing. All of this material, along with a check made out by Mom, was mailed to the Old San Francisco Mint Museum, which served as the U.S. Mint's order processing center during the 1970s.

Unlike today, when I can place an order online and possibly receive my Proof set in two or three days, back then, many months would pass before my set arrived via Registered Mail. There was an unbearable sense of anticipation when ripping open the extremely secure cardboard box used for shipping. Would I have a cameo set or not? To my delight, just as I was becoming aware of the desirability of cameo coins, the Mint began producing Proof coins that were likely to have at least some frosting on their devices most of the time. While the deep or ultra cameo contrast that we now take for granted did not appear until the end of the 1970s, I was satisfied with most of the sets of my youth.

To those who are just now discovering the exciting hobby of collecting Proof sets, and to those who are old hands like myself, this book is dedicated.

David W. Lange
Sarasota, Florida
March 2005

HISTORY OF PROOF SETS

The Early Years: U.S. Proofs in Their Infancy

The concept of Proof coins dates back hundreds of years, well before the establishment of the United States Mint in 1792. Newly created dies were given a fine polish, and a few coins were struck from them with great care for examination purposes. The engraver or coiner would inspect these first few coins to detect flaws in the dies. If any corrections were necessary, they would be made. If not, these pieces might very well be preserved as souvenirs of the occasion or placed into the national coin cabinet. Many nations maintained coin collections for centuries, and certain of these are still available for viewing by the public. In the case of kingdoms and other royal lands, coin collections that were formerly the property of a single ruler and his or her family have since become national collections. Proof specimens of coin types both adopted and rejected may be found within such collections.

The technological hurdles facing the infant United States Mint precluded such niceties as creating Proof examples of each and every coin type. It was challenging enough just to get its primitive machinery to produce coins of any quality, let alone Proofs. Nevertheless, superior specimens of some of our earliest federal coins are known. While these fall somewhat short of our current definition of Proof coins, they were clearly made from fresh and well-polished dies, and they were evidently struck with a bit of extra care as to centering, planchet quality, and strike sharpness.

Typically designated today as "specimen" strikes rather than Proofs, these coins are known for most of the designs adopted during the 1790s, silver dollars being the ones most likely to have survived to the present day. In the late 1790s, the Mint emphasized the utilitarian nature of coins, and little thought was given to striking coins of special beauty. For this reason, no specimen pieces were coined after about 1797 until the 1820s. Numismatists disagree about the status of some prooflike coins made during that interval. By 1821 (the earliest date for which a full Proof set, now in the Smithsonian Institution, is known), true Proofs were being made in very small numbers of selected dates and denominations.

People associated with the United States Mint and other government agencies typically preserved these specimen coins. Additional pieces were acquired by early visitors to the Philadelphia Mint, the only federal facility producing coins at that time. In a later era, a number of specimen coins have been repatriated from Europe, these pieces having been obtained during some long-ago visit to the young republic. There were quite a number of numismatists in Britain and Europe during this period, while there were very few in this country.

A handful of pioneer American collectors of coins and antiquities appeared during the early decades of the 19th century, these typically being men of wealth who possessed a broad range of scholarly interests. It was to be expected that they would sooner or later call on the Philadelphia Mint inquiring about the availability of Proof coins. The Mint had no formal program for producing and selling Proof coins before the 1850s, so a few pieces would simply be kept on hand or produced as needed for those who were interested. Sold at or just slightly above face value, the numbers distributed were extremely small, but this would soon change.

The discontinuation of large copper cents in 1857, in favor of the smaller diameter familiar today, induced a wave of nostalgia for the old coppers. This led to a frenzied rush to assemble complete runs of the available dates while they could still be found. This activity only fed a general trend that had been growing during the 1850s, as Americans sought to collect and study the coins of their grandparents' era. Proofs were now being routinely produced for all of the copper and silver coinage, though gold Proofs were seldom sought, due to their high face value.

As the number of requests for Proof coins grew, Mint Director James Ross Snowden sought to organize the coining and sales of Proofs in 1858 by publishing, for the first time, actual prices and ordering instructions. Sales of Proof coins really took off from that point, though mintages remained very low by modern standards. While no formal records were kept in the early years, sales seemed fairly consistent in relation to the numbers of each denomination distributed annually. Minor coins, which then consisted of cents, two-cent pieces (starting 1864), nickel three-cent pieces (starting 1865), and nickel five-cent pieces (starting 1866), typically enjoyed annual sales of about 1,500 to

2,000 Proofs. Silver coins, which included three-cent pieces and half dimes (both discontinued after 1873), dimes, twenty-cent pieces (1875 to 1878) quarters, halves, standard silver dollars (discontinued 1873), and trade dollars (1873 to 1883), had annual sales of roughly 500 to 1,000 coins. Gold coins, which, during some early years of public offering, could be ordered only in sets, and in other years singly, had ridiculously small sales of about 20 to 50 pieces each year. After about 1878, single Proofs could be ordered of the smaller denomination gold coins (dollar, quarter eagle, and $3), and these enjoyed somewhat higher sales. The quantity of large value (half eagle, eagle, and double eagle) gold Proofs, however, remained in the dozens.

The Early 1900s: A Booming Hobby

As the hobby grew during the second half of the 19th century, annual sales of Proof coins trended upward. This continued into the early 20th century, with the numbers of sets and singles sold increasing at a slow rate. Everything changed, however, with the introduction of radically different coin designs beginning in 1907. United States coins traditionally had flat fields that were easily polished to a brilliant finish. This contrasted nicely with the raised areas of the coins' designs, which had frosted textures. The combination of these brilliant and frosty surfaces resulted in a dual effect known as *cameo*, after the carved miniatures of similar contrast.

The new designs that appeared between 1907 and 1916 no longer had flat fields. Instead, their fields were convex in the die, thus concave on the coins struck from these dies. Without flat fields to polish to a brilliant finish, the Mint's coiners were at a loss on how to make Proofs. The solution was found in adopting the French Matte finish, so called because it was perfected at the Paris Mint. The new style of proofing created a coin with a uniformly granular finish that eliminated glare and permitted the viewer to take in every fine detail of the design. Today, these are generally grouped into several categories: Matte Proofs (Lincoln cents) 1909 to 1916 and Buffalo nickels of 1913 to 1916), Sand Blast Proofs (gold coins of 1908 and 1911 to 1915), and Satin Finish Proofs (gold coins of 1909 and 1910). Finishes such as these are said to have been highly regarded by medallists and art connoisseurs. Unfortunately, collectors of United States coins did not see their virtues, and there were numerous complaints amid declining Proof coin sales.

The introduction of new silver coin types in 1916 proved to be the final straw. It was intended that these designs be ready for the coin press early in 1916, and for that reason, the Mint did not coin Proofs of the old Liberty Head issues. Technical problems delayed production of new dimes, quarters, and halves until very late in the year, by which time it was too late to offer Proofs of either the old or new types. Because the new coin designs for silver denominations presented the same problems in proofing that the minor coins and gold coins did, and sales of those pieces had declined sharply, it was decided to discontinue Proof coin production and sales altogether after 1916. There were some appeals from collectors at the time to continue this program, but they were not sufficient to overcome resistance by the Treasury Department. America's entry into the World War in 1917 expanded an already great increase in the number of coins being made for circulation, so the likelihood of the Mint being able to devote time and resources to Proof production was slim, in any case.

There continued to be occasional calls for the resumption of Proof coin sales throughout the 1920s and early 1930s, but collectors of the time were remarkably disinterested in the then-current coin types that are so highly desired by hobbyists today. It was not until the notion of collecting coins from circulation, something nearly unknown before, swept the nation during the mid-1930s that an interest in current designs was sparked. The widespread marketing of inexpensive collecting boards for current or recent coin series created an entirely new generation of hobbyists that placed a much greater emphasis on modern rarities, such as the highly prized 1909-S V.D.B. cents.

As this generation grew in influence, a new hobby publication appeared which gave voice to their interests. *The Numismatic Scrapbook Magazine*, published by Lee and Clifford Hewitt in Chicago, debuted in 1935 and quickly became the journal of choice for this new generation of collectors. It was in the pages of this magazine that collectors followed the ongoing mania for current commemorative half dollars, a huge speculative market at that time, as well as the calls for a resumption of Proof coinage. Collectors wanted to have Proofs of the circulating issues that had never been coined in this manner, such as the Liberty Walking half dollar and the Mercury dime.

The Numismatic Scrapbook Magazine included this announcement:

[Treasury] Secretary Henry Morgenthau, Jr. on April 28th authorized the mint to resume the practice of striking Proof coins for the benefit of coin collectors.

According to press reports the suggestion to renew this practice was made by the late Louis McHenry Howe, secretary to President Roosevelt. Howe was said to have been interested in numismatics.

No Proofs of silver dollars will be made unless a substantial coinage is authorized later.

As the Proof set of 1936 was limited to coins then current, no gold Proofs were included. The set included the Lincoln cent, the Indian Head or Buffalo nickel, the Winged Liberty or "Mercury" dime, the Washington quarter, and the Liberty Walking half dollar. As in the past, Proofs could be purchased singly or as complete sets. Proof cents were priced at 16¢, nickels and dimes at 20¢, quarters at 50¢, and halves at 75¢. A complete set thus cost $1.81 when purchased in person at the Philadelphia Mint, or it could be ordered by mail for an additional cost of eight cents postage.

The first of the 1936-dated Proofs received by collectors displayed a uniform texture on both fields and devices and were less than fully brilliant. This texture has since been described by the hobby as a Satin Finish. The diminished brilliance was less noticeable on the silver pieces, that metal being naturally brilliant when polished, but the cents and nickels were another story. To the trained eye, these coins were clearly different from regular coins, but the many new coin collectors of that time complained that they were paying for coins not much better than the ones they could obtain at face value. This lament was hardly new, for a quarter century earlier, similar comments had been voiced concerning Matte Proof Lincoln cents and Buffalo nickels.

The American Numismatic Association's monthly journal, *The Numismatist*, could not ignore this popular outcry, and its editor, Frank G. Duffield, finally asked the Mint why Proof coins were not being delivered that had brilliant fields and frosted devices. Mint Director Nellie Tayloe Ross replied:

Your letter of June 13th, relative to Proof coins, has been referred to this Bureau for attention. The Superintendent submits the following explanation in regard to the method of preparing Proof coins:

Proof coins being struck at the mint at the present time are made in every detail exactly as they have been made in the past, namely, the planchets are carefully selected and each one struck individually on a hydraulic press, and handled so that one coin cannot mar another. The dies are polished to a mirror finish at frequent intervals.

The difference between the recent Proofs and those struck in the past is due to the difference in the design and the method used in preparing the master dies. All the present coins are made from sculptured models without retouching with a graver in any way in order to preserve the exact quality and texture of the original sculptor's work. This gives a more or less uneven background with less sharpness in the details. In other words, they are produced the same as small medals might be struck.

The master dies for the gold coins struck previous to 1907, and the silver coins struck prior to 1916, were prepared in the older and entirely different method, being lower in relief and much greater sharpness in detail by re-engraving, even though the original design was reduced from a sculptured model. The inscriptions were usually put in the master dies by means of punches. In addition, they were prepared with a "basined" background or field, that is, the field was polished to a perfect radius on a revolving disc, which again produced a much clearer definition between motif and field, and this gave an entirely different appearance to the coin.

With the present coins, the models were never prepared with the intention of "basining" and it could not be done without many radical alterations in the relief of the present designs.

While the issue of Proof coins having frosted relief elements was not resolved satisfactorily until the 1970s, the Proof coins struck later in the 1936 production were fully brilliant. This was noted at the time by popular writer Harry Boosel in his December 1937 column, "Capital Comment":

When the Mint at Philadelphia resumed striking Proofs last year, after a lapse of 20 years, the first efforts weren't acceptable to numismatists. Consequently, not many sets were sold. During the latter part of the year the mint improved the process, but not many knew it. Those Proofs that were coined late in 1936 were, in our opinion, every bit as good as those of the early years.

Proof coins were offered annually through 1942, as singles as well as complete sets. It seems that most collectors preferred the latter, with the cent and nickel enjoying some additional sales as singles. America's entry into World War II brought about a suspension in Proof coin sales. The number of coins being made for circulation increased several fold, while at the same time, there was a shortage of skilled labor at the mints. This prompted the issuance of a press release from the Superintendent's Office of the Philadelphia Mint early in 1943:

> In view of the extremely heavy demand for coinage and service medals, the facilities of the Mint are taxed almost beyond capacity. Due to this fact, the striking of Proof coins will necessarily be delayed for an indefinite period.

Collectors at the time did not anticipate that this suspension would last some five years beyond the war's end! A call for the resumption of Proof coin sales was almost immediate once peace returned, and this prompted the following response in 1946 to Stuart Mosher, editor of *The Numismatist*, from Leland Howard, acting director of the Mint:

> May we ask that you tell your readers not to write to the Treasury for the information? Both this office and the Philadelphia Mint (where Proofs are made) have been swamped with inquiries from interested persons. Your letter will be placed on file in order that you may be notified when plans for striking Proofs again are decided upon. In all probability nothing will be done until next year.

As we now know, nothing was done until 1950. The official explanation was that the Mint was still occupied to capacity in producing service medals for returning veterans, but there really was more to the story. In continued correspondence with Stuart Mosher, Acting Director Howard revealed that the Denver and San Francisco mints were actually operating *below* capacity. He emphasized, however, that these facilities had only electrical coining presses that were set up for a single striking of each planchet at high speeds, rather than the slow, multiple strikings required of Proof coins. Further, he reassured Mosher and his readers that the Mint's production of coins for other countries was not a cause for the delay in Proof coin production.

Eventually, with enough probing, the real reason that Proofs were not being made was revealed. Mosher learned that the issue was budgetary. After the many social programs of the 1930s, followed by several years of high military spending during the war, the federal budget was slashed heavily during the late 1940s, and this cost-cutting had caught up to the Mint, too. Its annual appropriation was reduced in proportion, and this simply left no money for producing collector coins. While it may seem today that the profits from Proof set sales more than justified the production of such coins, the fact is that any profits went into the Treasury Department's general fund and were thus not credited to the Mint. This left the Mint with no money to produce Proof coins in advance of sales. This problem, in one form or another, dogged the Mint as late as the 1980s, though today the Mint has an enterprise fund that permits it to operate more like a business than a governmental agency.

On February 25, 1949, a bill was finally introduced into the Senate to permit the Mint to retain its Proof coin profits to the extent needed to offset their expenses, the remaining profits to be turned over to the Treasury. The Senate passed the bill in July, but it was not until May 2, 1950, that the House of Representatives finally approved it. Acting Director Howard personally telephoned ANA President M. Vernon Sheldon with the good news, and President Harry S Truman signed the bill into law on May 10, 1950.

The Late 1900s and Beyond: Improvements and Perfection

The sale of Proof coins dated 1950 began on July 17 of that year. These coins would be available only in complete sets of five pieces, the cost for each set being $2.10. A temporary limit of five sets per customer was imposed, though this ultimately proved unnecessary, as sales for the year totaled just 51,386 sets.

The new Proof sets included the Roosevelt dime and the Franklin half dollar, but they were otherwise quite similar in design to the Proofs of 1936 to 1942. Many of the 1950-dated Proofs had satiny finishes similar to those of early 1936, and it seems the Mint had to once again learn how to produce mirror-finish Proofs. A few of the 1951 Proofs were likewise of diminished brilliance, but the Mint's coiners soon adopted pre-war techniques, and the Proofs of 1952 and later are fully brilliant.

While it was ideal that these Proofs have frosted portraits and lettering, the Proof-making techniques employed at the time weighed against it. Only the first few Proofs struck from new dies displayed such frosting, which was quickly abraded from the die cavities as the metal-to-metal contact produced a self-polishing effect. The result was just a handful of deeply frosted Proofs from each die, followed by perhaps a few dozen that revealed ever diminishing degrees of frosting, until the remainder of the press run included only coins that were uniformly brilliant on both fields and devices. These comprise the majority of Proofs manufactured 1936 to 1970. Later on, techniques were developed which preserved this frosting for longer periods. Still later, it was preserved for the entire span of a Proof die's utility.

In the 1950s, dies intended for Proof coin production were carefully cleaned before being dipped in a solution of 5% nitric acid and 95% alcohol. This gently "pickled" the entire face of the die, creating a subtle frosting effect throughout. The fields of the die were then polished with a diamond dust compound using a wooden mandrel, or rotary tool, followed up by a finishing polish with a felt mandrel. This created the two-toned effect known as "cameo" that is so desired by collectors.

Planchets (coin blanks) intended for Proof coins were subjected to the normal cleaning processes used for regular coining. They then also burnished by being tumbled inside a cylindrical drum filled with small steel beads. After that, they were washed in an Ivory® soap solution and towel-dried. After that point, following a quick visual inspection for cleanliness, they were ready for the press.

Slow action presses were used to strike Proof coins two or three times, providing them with a full and even impression. Proof coins were, and still are today, removed from the press very carefully to prevent contact with other coins. While this process used to be performed by employees using their gloved hands or a pair of tongs, it is now done automatically by machines.

As collectors became more aware of the superior-quality products being offered by other nations, particularly the superb coins being made at Canada's Ottawa Mint, they began to call for greater perfection in the U.S.A.'s Proof coins. The U.S. Mint answered this call beginning in the late 1960s with improved die and planchet preparation techniques. The dies, instead of being pickled in acid, were now sandblasted to produce a deeper frosting. The dies were then covered with clear tape that was carefully trimmed, masking the die cavities to protect their precious frosting while exposing the fields to the polishing process that followed. After the fields were polished to a brilliant mirror finish, the entire die face was then chromium-plated to preserve its cameo effect. When Proof dies began to show signs of wear, those that were deemed still fit for Proof coins were stripped of their chromium plating, and the entire process described above was repeated.

The preparation of planchets was improved by rinsing them in a gentle acid solution to remove any impurities before they were once again cleaned. This combination of superior dies and planchets has resulted in the nearly perfect Proofs typical since the late 1970s. The entire process is described in greater detail in Rick Tomaska's excellent book, *Cameo and Brilliant Proof Coinage of the 1950 to 1970 Era*.

Such improvements, however, were far in the future for collectors of Proof sets during the 1950s and early '60s. The sets remained somewhat similar year after year, though the number of cameo coins increased starting in 1960. This was little-appreciated by collectors of the time, who placed more emphasis on completion of their sets than on the quality of individual pieces. The popularity of Proof coins rose alongside a general burst of hobby activity that peaked around 1963-1964, but the numismatic hobby suffered several shocks beginning in 1964 that led to both a suspension of Proof set sales and a general decline in the popularity of coin collecting. It was not until the late 1990s that the coin hobby would again experience a massive influx of new collectors.

A shortage of coins in general circulation began to develop around 1961, and this reached crisis proportions by the end of 1963. At a loss to explain the phenomenon, and clearly on the defensive from a hostile press and Congress, Mint Director Eva Adams took the unprecedented action of placing the blame on coin collectors! It was no secret that the hobby was very popular at the time, as coin collecting themes worked their way into the mass media as never before. While the numbers of coins held by hobbyists could in no way account for the national shortage, collectors became the convenient scapegoats.

Among the many radical steps undertaken to address the coin shortage was a suspension of the use of mintmarks on all coins until further notice. Also authorized was retention of the date 1964 on coins beyond that calendar year. It was believed that these combined actions would serve to make current coins so undesirable to collectors that they would stop their alleged hoarding of them. Coming at the same time, though not directly related, was the abandonment of silver in the dime and quarter and the significant reduction of this metal in the half dollar. Coins of these new compositions were introduced in stages between November 1965 and April 1966, the halves being the last to debut.

Because the minting facilities in use at that time were so busy with this replacement coinage, Mint Director Adams announced that there would be no Proof coins made or sold after 1964 until further notice. Neither, it was revealed, would the Mint offer its annual Uncirculated sets consisting of one each of the regular coins from the Denver and Philadelphia mints. As may be imagined, this did not sit well with collectors, who were already being punished on several fronts. A compromise of sorts was reached early in 1966 when the Mint announced the introduction of Special Mint Sets, a hybrid coinage that would be better than the quality of circulating pieces but not equal to true Proofs. The following press release was dated March 8, 1966:

> Coins in the new sets will be struck one at a time from specially prepared blanks, on high tonnage presses, and handled individually after striking. The will have a higher relief than regular coins and be better in appearance than any of the regular Uncirculated sets heretofore issued. All coins in the new sets will be dated 1965. The will not carry mintmarks.
>
> The Special Mint Sets will be sold in lots of one, two, five, or ten sets, only, to a customer. They will be made at the San Francisco Assay Office.

It turned out that these sets were produced for the years 1965 through 1967, after which time the sale of normal Proof sets resumed. The SMS coins, despite the Mint's assurances, do not appear to have been made with any great care. While they are more brilliant than the regular coinage, they tend to show numerous marks and light abrasions. Some of these marks were on the planchets prior to coining. The multiple impressions typical of Proof coins would have flattened them out as the planchets filled the dies fully. SMS coins, however, appear to have been struck just once, leaving these flaws visible on the finished coins.

The 1965 SMS coins, which were actually produced in 1966, come with a finish either satiny or brilliant. This is akin to the Proofs of 1936 and 1950, and it did nothing to endear these coins to collectors. While the 1966 and 1967 sets are closer in appearance to actual Proofs, they are found with numerous flaws that prevent them from being graded highly by third-party certification services. In addition, cameo examples are quite rare, as the dies for these coins were not prepared with the same care as those for true Proofs. The final insult was that the price for each set was $4, nearly a 100% increase from the $2.10 price of the 1950 through 1964 Proof sets.

The Mint did make one concession to collectors in the form of improved packaging. While the 1965 SMS was delivered in the same flexible plastic bag used for Proof sets since 1955, the 1966-1967 sets were sealed in an attractive holder of rigid plastic that offered greater protection to the coins.

In late 1967, the Mint announced that the great coin shortage was over and that the emergency measures put into effect as a result of it would be lifted in 1968. With the return of mintmarks to our coins came also the return of Proof sets. The San Francisco Assay Office had proved quite satisfactory at making and packaging the SMS products, so the production of Proof coins for general distribution was moved there from Philadelphia for the first time in the U.S. Mint's history.

The 1968 Proof set, containing five coins bearing the S mintmark of San Francisco, was priced at $5, considered by collectors a fairly steep price at the time. The Mint justified this increase by pointing to its attractive and convenient new plastic holder for the sets. An advance from the SMS plastic holders of 1966-1967, it featured frosted borders and raised print on the cover. The greater cost of this set also included delivery by Registered Mail, a step imposed because so many of the 1964 Proof sets had been stolen during shipment.

Collectors were pleased with the new sets, ordering far more than the San Francisco Assay Office could produce and quickly running up the after-market price to $15 and more. Part of their appeal was that they included three coins not available as circulating issues: the Proof-only S-Mint dime, quarter, and half. After 1970, the San Francisco nickel was likewise a Proof-only coin, and the cent would follow after 1974.

Proof sets remained very popular with collectors, typically selling around three million sets per year. Their aesthetic value improved during the 1970s, as the advanced technology described previously led to more consistently frosted Proofs. The introduction of the Eisenhower dollar into the Proof set in 1973, followed shortly thereafter by the three U.S.A. Bicentennial coins, kept interest in Proof sets high throughout the decade. In 1979, the much-heralded Anthony dollar appeared and was immediately included in that year's Proof set. Though the coin failed as a circulating medium, it was quite popular with collectors until its coinage was suspended in 1982 (to be resumed briefly years later in 1999).

These were years of relatively high monetary inflation by American standards, with the annual inflation rate hitting double digits by 1980. The issue price of the U.S. Mint's Proof sets kept pace with these advances, reaching $11 by 1981, where it remained for the next decade. By this time, Proof sets having fully frosted lettering and devices and nearly flawless surfaces were the norm. These are coins that today are being certified by third-party grading services as either "Ultra Cameo" (used by Numismatic Guaranty Corporation of America) or "Deep Cameo" (used by Professional Coin Grading Service). These terms mean exactly the same thing, and they describe coins that have superb contrast between brilliant fields and richly frosted devices.

During the 1980s, no new coin types were introduced, and the U.S. Mint's Proof sets fell into a regular pattern that left each year's set looking exactly like the one preceding it. Color schemes changed a bit in the packaging (this is described more fully in the date-by-date analysis chapter), but in most respects there was a certain sameness to these sets. Collector interest began to lag by the early 1990s, so something new was needed to revitalize it.

The U.S. Mint's bicentennial in 1992 should have been the occasion for a set of commemorative coins, but instead just a medal was offered, and even this used components adapted from previous issues. Collectors were rightfully disappointed, though the fault lay not with the Mint, which was unable to change coin designs without Congressional approval. Still, the Mint sought to offer collectors a more fitting souvenir of this memorable anniversary. Fortunately, a bill was passed that permitted the Mint to create and sell Proof examples of the dime, quarter, and half in their historic composition of 90% silver, and 10% copper, which had last been used in 1964.

In 1992, the Mint thus offered the regular five-coin Proof set featuring copper-nickel clad dimes, quarters, and halves, as well as five-coin sets in which these three denominations were made of "coin silver." While the regular Proof set was still priced at $11 (raised to $12.50 the following year), the silver Proof set was priced at $21. Both sets included the normal Proof cents and nickels, so collectors ordering one of each set found themselves with duplicates of these coins.

Also offered in 1992 were silver Premier Proof sets at $37, which were simply the same coins found in the silver Proof set but with deluxe packaging. To these three sets were added the U.S. Mint's Prestige Proof sets, an option that had been offered irregularly since 1983. The contents of the Prestige Proof sets varied from year to year, but they included the five regular Proof coins and one or two issues from that year's commemorative program. Their prices varied from one edition to the next, ranging as high as $59 and as low as $45. Prestige Proof sets and silver Premier Proof sets enjoyed only limited sales, and both programs were discontinued in the late 1990s.

It was uncertain at the time whether the Mint would continue to offer a silver Proof set after the bicentennial year of 1992, but the success of this program prompted its continuance to the present day. Sales of these sets, as well as those of the regular copper-nickel clad Proof sets, were modest in the years 1993 to 1998, but they rebounded mightily with the introduction of the 50 State Quarters® Program in 1999.

Congress authorized this ten-year program in which the regular reverse of John Flanagan's Washington quarter would be replaced with a series of commemorative reverses honoring the nation's fifty states. Since 1999, states have been recognized with designs of their own choosing, at the rate of five states per year. Still ongoing at this time, the program is scheduled to conclude after 2008, unless it is extended for the inclusion of America's commonwealth and protectorate entities such as Puerto Rico, Guam, and American Samoa. The District of Columbia, too, wants to be recognized with a commemorative quarter design.

Current Proof sets are offered in several options. The ten-coin, regular Proof set features the year's five statehood quarters in copper-nickel clad composition, as well as the five remaining denominations current. This includes the recent Sacagawea dollar, first minted in 2000. The five-piece clad Proof set is also available each year for those who want only the state quarters. Beginning in 2004, a five-piece set of the silver state quarters was added as an option. Finally, a complete Proof set of ten coins, featuring the dime, half dollar, and five state quarters in historical 90% silver, is offered annually.

The enormous and widespread popularity of this program has prompted a resurgence of popular coin collecting unseen since the early 1960s, when silver coins were still circulating. Substantial mintages are being recorded for the both the clad and silver Proof sets featuring state quarters, yet the demand for these coins seems unlimited at the present time. The first few years of state quarter Proof sets have witnessed remarkable price advances for these coins in both their original Mint packaging and as individual pieces certified and encapsulated by third-party grading services. A very recent development has been the certification and encapsulation of complete Proof sets within a single holder by Numismatic Guaranty Corporation.

The rise in interest prompted by the 50 State Quarters® Program has been extended to all Proof sets of the modern era, with a particular emphasis on those issued during the 1980s and '90s. Because sales were lagging during those years, some of these sets seem to have been bargains compared to current price levels. Whether or not this degree of interest is sustained beyond the conclusion of the 50 State Quarters® Program in 2008 remains to be seen. One thing is certain, however: Proof sets minted since 1936 have always been and will continue to be collector favorites.

COLLECTING AND
STORING PROOF SETS

Collecting Over the Years

The notion of a complete Proof set is commonplace today, as we are familiar with purchasing these sets annually from the U.S. Mint already mounted as a set. In the early years of American numismatics, however, this concept was somewhat alien. Proof coins were acquired as singles prior to 1858, the year that the Mint first solicited orders from the public, and it was not always the case that every denomination was made in Proof form. For example, Proofs are known for most minor coins and silver coins for the years immediately preceding 1858, but the coining of gold Proofs was a hit and miss affair, with many gaps existing in the date sequence.

From 1858 onward, it is a safe assumption that all denominations coined at the Philadelphia Mint were obtainable as Proofs, with the notable exception of commemorative coins. In some rare instances, such as the nickels of 1877 and 1878, only Proofs were made. This situation lasted through 1915, at which time the last Proofs were made of the gold and silver coins. Only cents and nickels were offered as Proofs the following year, and then sales of Proof coins were suspended altogether for some twenty years.

From 1858 through 1915, the annual purchase of Proof minor and silver coins was standard practice for many collectors of current issues. Many speculators acquired additional sets of the minor pieces (cent through nickel), as there were always new collectors entering the market. There was some additional interest in Proofs of the gold dollar, quarter eagle, and $3 gold piece, as these, too, were subject to speculative trading. But gold Proofs of higher denominations were in far less demand, and their tiny sales reflected this fact. When offered at auction, a Proof double eagle might realize less than face value after the commission was deducted!

When Proof coins reappeared in 1936, collectors initially took little notice of them. This situation was aggravated as reports from early purchasers indicated that the cents and nickels were not as brilliant as one would expect. Though the Mint quickly corrected this feature to everyone's satisfaction, the sales of 1936 sets were somewhat disappointing. Nevertheless, each year's sales were above those of the year before, and by 1938, there were already enough new enthusiasts that the 1936 sets were rising in value. The sales of Proof sets rose dramatically in 1941 and 1942, before America's entry into World War II saw them suspended once again.

When sales resumed in 1950, the story was much the same as in 1936. Collectors seemed to take a wait-and-see attitude toward the new sets. The U.S. Mint had to relearn the Proof making process, and the 1950 sets varied widely in quality. The 1951 Proof coins, too, were of variable quality, many having satiny or semi-brilliant finishes. Despite this inauspicious beginning, interest in Proof sets began to rise steadily with the hobby boom that began in 1952. Sales rose accordingly, and a speculative market in Proof sets quickly developed.

This reached a fever pitch in 1956 and 1957, with the 1936 through 1942 sets, and even the sets from 1950 onward, rising in value to many multiples of issue price. Proof sets were being viewed more like commodities than collectibles, being traded in quantity several times daily during the height of the market. At least one dealer took a blackboard to coin shows upon which he wrote his buy and sell prices, these being updated with each new report on the market.

As with all speculative bubbles, the inevitable happened, and the market burst. This occurred when the Mint released its sales figures for the 1957 Proof set. At more than a million sets delivered, this was a blow to the perception that Proof sets were something rare. It was a figure that would be exceeded time and again in years to come, but in 1957, the coin market simply was not ready to digest it.

The Proof set market ultimately recovered and enjoyed several years of relative stability, while speculator interest shifted toward rolls and bags of Uncirculated coins from recent years back to 1934. Though this speculation, centering on coins made in the tens or even hundreds of millions, made far less sense than the mania for Proof sets, it held sway over the American hobby scene from the late 1950s through 1964.

In that latter year, the debut of the wildly popular Kennedy half dollar created a renewed rush for Proof sets that saw nearly four million produced. Proof set speculation focused upon this single date, driving up the price of that very common set to an unnatural level for a few years. The Special Mint Sets offered in lieu of Proof sets during 1965 to 1967 generated little interest at the time, and this writer remembers them selling for less than issue price for many years.

When Proof sets reappeared in 1968, this time bearing the magical S mintmark of San Francisco, the frenzy to buy as many sets as possible resulted in another illogical price climb. Issued at $5 per set, this quickly rose to $15 on the secondary market, yet collectors could not get enough of them. Once the speculation had ended, however, this was another set that could be obtained for years afterward for $3 to $4. Like all these sets from the 1960s, it has since crept back up in value, though perhaps not enough to keep up with inflation.

Other Proof sets that have elicited speculative attention and attendant price rises are those from 1970 (no circulating halves), 1973 (the first cupronickel-clad Proof Ike dollar), 1975 (the first year of Proof-only S-Mint cents), 1976 (the U.S.A. Bicentennial coins), 1981 (the last Anthony dollar, or so we thought at the time), and 1986 (a lower than normal mintage).

The first of the modern silver Proof sets in 1992 generated some excitement at the time, though later sets have proved to be more valuable in the after market. Perhaps the biggest news to affect the collecting and trading of Proof sets has been the 50 State Quarters® Program that began in 1999 and is still ongoing. More new collectors of Proof sets have come into the hobby in these few years than in the thirty years previous.

Some Options For Collecting

The modern Proof set series that began in 1936 is now a very long one, encompassing hundreds of different coins. Some of these have become quite valuable, particularly in the higher grades. For most collectors, however, the completion of a Proof series from 1936 to the present is still an attainable goal. Whether one seeks coins in their original packaging (becoming quite rare for 1950 to 1954 sets and nearly impossible for 1936 to 1942 sets) or attempts to purchase only third-party certified coins, opportunities abound.

These are various options available to the collector who might not feel the need to assemble a complete series of Proof coins all the way back to 1936. In the case of Proof sets, each one is a small, collectible item in its own right. While many collectors will still desire to own each and every Proof set of the modern era, from 1936 to date, others will be satisfied to start their series with 1950 or, perhaps, with 1968.

Another option is to acquire Proof sets that represent the various design changes. For example, a Proof set of 1936 or 1937 would be needed to illustrate the Buffalo nickel, and this would likewise take care of the Mercury dime and Liberty Walking half dollar. A second set, from the 1950s, will include the Roosevelt dime and Franklin half dollar. A 1964 Proof set would be a welcome addition in illustrating the Lincoln Memorial cent and Kennedy half dollar.

Continuing onward, a Proof set from 1973 or 1974 features the Eisenhower dollar, while a 1975 or 1976 set includes the three U.S.A. Bicentennial coins. A Proof set from the years 1979 to 1981 illustrates the ill-fated Anthony dollar, while the sets from 1999 onward feature five different state quarters in each set. Those dated 2000 and later also include the handsome Sacagawea dollar, which, sadly, appears to be suffering the same fate of unpopularity as the Anthony dollar. Such sets would fit nicely into a general collection of United States coins by design types, a popular pursuit.

Mint Packaging

While United States Proof sets have been produced continually from 1858 to 1916, intermittently to 1964, and continually since 1968, it has only been in recent decades that the U.S. Mint paid much attention to its own packaging of these coins. Since 1968, the Mint has delivered all of its Proof sets in rigid plastic holders that both display the coins in an attractive manner and offer excellent protection from contact and environmental damage. While the degree of safety may be affected by the storage environment one selects for his or her collection, the Proof set holders themselves provide a relatively stable home.

This evolutionary development, however, was a long time coming. The collector of 1858 received Proof coins in, at most, folded individual tissues. These coins could be purchased in person from the Philadelphia Mint's medals clerk, or they could be ordered by mail. In either case, the coin was packaged with only the slightest protection from mishandling. It was up to the collector to devise a long-term means of storage for the Proof coins.

These tissues remained in general use by the Mint until Proof coin sales were suspended in 1916. Twenty years later, in 1936, Proofs were once again offered to the public as either single pieces or complete sets of five coins. Instead of tissue, however, each coin was placed within a small cellophane sleeve, and the sleeves stapled together at the top for orders of two or more coins. While similar in form to the polyethylene sleeves still used in the hobby today, these early products were more chemically reactive and often toned the coins. The cellophane envelope had glued seams, and the seam line often transmitted a gray or black line to the coins, especially those in silver. Most commonly seen is a somewhat milky haze that is light tan in color. While some collectors like to see this toning as a sign of originality, the irregular shape it often assumes does not appeal to most.

Proof set sales were suspended after 1942, due to the war effort, and they resumed in 1950. Only complete, five-coin sets were offered thereafter, but the packaging remained similar. The five sleeves were stapled together at one end or corner, and this bundle was placed inside a small cardboard box. Crumpled paper was used to limit the sleeves' movement within the box, which was then taped shut. Each boxed set was packaged within a larger box for mailing, according to how many sets were ordered.

Cellophane sleeves were used through 1953, but these were replaced the following year with polyethylene. This reduced the hairlines scratches often caused by the coarser 1936 through 1953 sleeves, and it also imparted an odd, purplish toning to many of the 1954 and 1955 Proofs.

Midway through the 1955 deliveries, the U.S. Mint switched to a different packaging altogether. The "box set" was replaced with the more appealing "flat pack" in which all five coins and a Mint label were heat-sealed between two sheets of transparent polyethylene. Each coin was held in place within its own window formed by the heat sealing pattern, which permitted viewing of the entire coin. The sealed set was then placed within a paper envelope of similar size that also included a fact sheet about the set. The sealed envelope could be sold by the Mint as it was, or, for multiple set orders, placed within a mailing box.

The flat pack remained standard packaging for all Proof sets through 1964 and for the Special Mint Sets of 1965. In 1966, however, the Mint responded to the growing popularity of rigid plastic holders offered by the commercial sector by devising a rigid holder of its own. These were used for the SMS coins of 1966 and 1967 and presented a very attractive display. The more elaborate packaging also went a long way toward alleviating collector frustration with the price increase that accompanied introduction of the Special Mint Sets.

A further advance was made with the framed picture format used for the Proof sets starting in 1968. In one form or another, this basic concept has been retained ever since. Detailed descriptions of the U.S. Mint's Proof set packaging will be found in the chapter that studies each set by date.

Other Storage and Display Options

The attractiveness and protection offered by the Mint's Proof set packaging since 1968 has nearly eliminated the market for commercially made Proof set holders. Some marketers still manage to entice collectors to remount their sets within holders that include a space for baby photos, wedding photos, and the like, but the number of Mint-sealed sets being broken open for that purpose seems to be minimal. A far greater challenge to the survival of original U.S. Mint packaging is the widespread popularity of third-party grading and encapsulation. As an employee of Numismatic Guaranty Corporation, this writer has witnessed many thousands of sets being taken apart for grading and encapsulation within NGC's own holders.

In the 21st century, we are inundated with safe and attractive products for storing and displaying coins. Such was the not the case, however, during American numismatics' first century. A collector living in 1860, 1900, or even 1930 had precious few options for storing coins, and none of these offered much protection from the environment. This accounts for the great number of Proof coins seen today that display hairline scratches, small nicks, and other flaws that serve to diminish their grades.

A wealthy numismatist of the 19th and early 20th centuries typically would store coins in a fine wooden cabinet made for that specific purpose. These looked like oversized jewelry boxes, and they contained numerous shallow drawers or trays. Each drawer was a laminate of two or more panels of wood, the uppermost panel being cut with holes of varying diameters to accommodate coins or medals of different sizes. Within each hole was felt or some other soft lining upon which the coins rested, their facing surfaces being exposed to the air until the drawer was closed.

In most collections, the uppermost drawers were cut for small size coins or medalets, while the diameters of the holes increased from top to bottom. This placed the largest and heaviest numismatic items lower in the cabinet, which increased its stability. Most coin cabinets rested firmly atop some larger piece of furniture, but the more ornate ones stood upon their own legs and were subject to tipping if their center of gravity was too high.

Coin cabinets offered good protection from contact with other coins and medals, provided those handling such pieces did not drop them! Unfortunately, they offered little in the way of protection from chemical reaction with the atmosphere. Most coin collectors of the time lived in coal-powered Eastern and Midwestern cities; this resulted in coins that became deeply toned on the exposed side, while the side that rested against the soft lining material was masked from exposure. A collector could correct for this by periodically turning the coins over to balance their toning, but with more handling came an increased risk of imparting hairline scratches from movement of the coins against the lining. Such hairlines were known to earlier generations of collectors and catalogers as "cabinet friction."

Further down the economic scale were collectors who lacked either the means or the space for a fine wooden cabinet. Prior to about 1930, their only other option was to place their coins within small envelopes. These typically measured two inches square and were made of heavy kraft paper. Their lightweight descendants are still used in the coin hobby today, though now they are just a small segment of the coin supply market.

Even some of the more affluent collectors opted to use these envelopes, since they provided a large area for writing descriptions, acquisition dates, and sources. While inexpensive and fairly easy to store in boxes, these envelopes offered nothing in the way of protection from atmospheric contaminants and harmful sliding of the coins within. Indeed, the very material from which these envelopes were made was itself harmful, being rich in chemically reactive sulfur. A partial solution was found in the marketing of "anti-tarnish" tissues by Aubrey Bebee, the Hewitt Brothers, and other vendors, starting in the 1930s. Coins were placed within these tissues before being inserted into envelopes, thus offering a chemical barrier that proved moderately successful. In recent decades, these tissues have been supplanted by cotton liners or polyethylene sleeves that serve the same purpose.

Whether one used coin cabinets or envelopes, a common problem existed in that coins were difficult to display and share with others, particularly non-collectors who lacked knowledge of how to handle them properly. Here the situation remained until the late 1920s, when Martin Luther Beistle invented the ancestor of the now familiar coin album. Beistle was a manufacturer of seasonal paper novelties, such as holiday decorations and party hats, but he was also a collector of coins. He used his company's tooling to devise a coin panel that both stored and displayed coins in relative safety.

Its construction was quite simple: a panel of heavy cardboard measuring 7½ inches wide by 14 inches high was lined on the front and back with sheets of paper that were glued to it at selected points. A series of holes corresponding in diameter to the coins that would be mounted within the panel was punched through all three pieces. Then, slides of transparent acetate were slid between the cardboard and its paper coverings to hold the coins in place. Thus, the coins could be viewed both obverse and reverse while being held securely within their holes. Each panel was punched in its left margin for mounting within a three-ring binder, which the Beistle Company also supplied. By 1931, Beistle had sold his invention to prominent coin dealer Wayte Raymond, who marketed it as The National Coin Album. This series of albums was quite popular for decades, and old collections still appear within them from time to time.

Later manufacturers improved upon Beistle's simple design, reshaping the panels into more convenient sizes, adding attractive graphic features, and providing more appealing, book-like bindings. The coin album soon became the method of choice for storing one's better coins, and it predominated through the 1960s. In a period when most collectors sought complete sets by date and mint, Proofs were often substituted for the currency strikes of the Philadelphia Mint coinage in such albums. The popularity of the flat pack Proof sets of 1955 through 1964 prompted a couple of album manufacturers to produce titles in which the pages featured large, rectangular openings for the display of such sets within their original packaging.

Albums have some drawbacks, however, in that coins are exposed to cardboard on their edges, while careless movement of the plastic slides may impart hairline scratches on a coin's high points. Though they remain popular today, coin albums now must compete with a variety of single-coin and multi-coin holders.

For those on an even lower budget, inexpensive coin boards appeared shortly after the debut of albums—in 1934, to be exact. With coin boards, there were no slides. The backside of the cardboard panel was lined with paper, while coins were simply pressed into the holes until they came to rest against this backing paper. This left the obverse of the coin exposed to atmospheric contaminants, while the reverse was subjected to whatever chemicals were present in the paper and in the glue used to affix it to the cardboard panel.

A few years later, these 11 inches wide by 14 inches high coin boards were replaced with coin folders. Using the same materials, the single, large panel was replaced with two or three smaller ones that folded over one another to form a booklet. This somewhat reduced atmospheric exposure, but it still left the coins in contact with dried glue and sulfurous paper. Even in the 1930s, experienced collectors recognized that such products were not suitable for delicate Proof coins, though coin boards and folders introduced many new collectors to the hobby.

World War II prompted a great increase in the popularity of coin collecting, as Americans were working overtime shifts and earning a lot of money for which they had few recreational outlets. The production of most non-essential consumer goods had been suspended, and it seemed that nearly everything was being rationed. Both stamp collecting and coin collecting enjoyed a boom during the war years, through 1948, after which an economic recession temporarily diminished this excitement.

The war had likewise brought some great advances in technology, particularly in the field of plastics. Though Americans were already familiar with celluloid, bakelite, and nylon—all developed before the war—now there was a variety of synthetic materials that offered unlimited opportunities to the manufacturing sector.

By 1945, this revolution had already touched the coin hobby. LeRoy Kurtzeborn and Paul Seitz were pioneers in the offering of rigid plastic holders for the display of single and multiple coins. Their holders featured panels of acrylic plastic held together by screws of either metal or plastic. Such holders could contain single coins, a complete five-piece Proof set, or an entire series of coins. These products were similar in appearance to holders still being made today and were often used for displaying Proof sets dated 1936 through 1964 at a time when the U.S. Mint's own packaging was primitive in comparison. From the 1950s through the 1980s, such display holders competed about evenly with coin albums in the hobby market. It was only with the onset of third-party grading and encapsulation that they began to be seen less often.

Indeed, the introduction of encapsulated grading that began with Professional Coin Grading Service (PCGS) in 1986, Numismatic Guaranty Corporation of America (NGC) in 1987 and ANACS in 1989 has changed the hobby in many ways. Not only has this standardized grading for most dealers and collectors, but also it has changed the way in which collectors collect. The popularity of certified coins within individual holders has challenged the very notion of collecting complete series by date and mint, a concept that had been central to the American coin market since Augustus Heaton published his treatise on the virtues of branch mint coins in 1893.

Collectors of today are much more inclined to look at each coin purchase as a stand-alone item, not feeling the same urge to have one of everything that was so common to earlier generations. Of course, the expense of assembling a high-grade series of the older coin types has something to do with this, too. That explains the current appeal of more recent series such as Roosevelt dimes and Eisenhower dollars, as these can be completed on a middle-class budget.

Even "slab" collectors have some options when it comes to displaying their coins. The major grading services offer plastic boxes that hold about 15 to 20 of their certified and encapsulated coins. A search through the advertisements in popular hobby publications will reveal some other options for certified coins that are more akin to the old album concept. Pages are offered that hold various numbers of slabbed coins that fit into attractive ring binders made to suit. Various products reminiscent of the sliding drawers found in antique coin cabinets are also available. While typically a bit more expensive, these offer a deluxe presentation for one's better coins.

One alternative for those who preferred certified and encapsulated coins, but who also wish to maintain their Proof sets as sets, is a product created by Numismatic Guaranty Corporation of America in 2003. This is NGC's Multi-Coin holder, in which up to six coins may be encapsulated within a single holder comprised of materials quite similar to those used for NGC's single coin encapsulation. Each coin is given a certified grade, whether a single matching grade for the entire set or a listing of the individual grades within a single label. This option combines the completeness of a Proof set with the guarantee and environmental protection of a certified holder.

A recent development that seems to be countering the trend away from the collecting of complete sets is the popularity of online certified collection registries. These registries may be described as "virtual coin collections," though the coins posted on them are quite real. Both PCGS and NGC host online registries that are open to collectors and dealers alike. The only significant difference between the two is that PCGS limits its registry to coins it has certified, while NGC's registry accepts both NGC and PCGS coins. Neither uncertified coins nor those or other grading services are presently accepted in these registries.

Each registry features a variety of set options for either complete date series (such as Lincoln Cents from 1909 to date) or partial sets (such as the Lincoln Memorial series from 1959 to date). Different set options are available for Proof or circulating coins, while some additional sets are offered that permit both issues. Once a user has registered online, he may create his own collection within the chosen registry set option. After entering the desired name for his collection, such as "John Doe's Beautiful Proof Lincolns," he may then register each coin in the collection by entering its certified identification number as it appears on the grading label. The registry has a pre-assigned score for each date and mint combination in the various possible grades. Thus, the score value of each coin entered, as well as the total score value of the set, is calculated automatically. Users can view the scoring tables at any time, permitting them to predict the effect that upgrading will have upon their set and its placement relative to those of other users.

Available also are the options of including electronic images of one's coins, as well as providing a brief narrative for each coin and for the collection as a whole. In this respect, certified collection registries have partially supplanted the displaying of one's collection at a coin show or club meeting. While some collectors continue to enjoy both venues for exhibiting, those who are unable to travel to shows or who are reluctant to risk displaying their collections publicly have found the online certified registries to be the perfect alternative.

While some collectors register their sets online just for the pleasure of sharing them with others, such a display also provides a pleasurable alternative to having one's coins at home, where they lack the safety afforded by a bank vault or other secure facility. The user may view his collection at any time with a few clicks of the mouse, while knowing that the actual coins are safely tucked away.

Competition is another appeal of online registries, as the total score of one's set determines its rank relative to those entered by other users in that same category. Having a first- or second-place registry set is quite a status symbol, one that is often touted when these collections come up for sale. In fact, it's not unusual for registry collections to be sold either publicly or privately soon after achieving this status. Much of the pleasure in owning the coins seems to revolve around having beaten out other, similar collections within the online registries. With nowhere higher to go, some owners soon lose interest in that particular series and will use the proceeds from a collection's sale to begin yet another competitive registry collection.

Registries seem to have become particularly attractive to collectors of modern Proof coins, an area in which just a single grade point can mean the difference between being number one and being number two. Information about these online certified coin registries is available at the NGC and PCGS web sites.

Building a Proof Coin Set

Described above were some options for assembling a series of Proof sets, starting with 1936, 1950, 1965, or 1968. But what about the coins themselves? Which grades should one choose? What features should one look for when selecting just the right coin?

To some degree, this is a question that varies with the starting date of one's Proof series. Proof coins of the years 1936 to 1942 are collectible in grades as low as PF-63. Even so, while such a grade may still be desirable for the most expensive coins in these sets, such as the Buffalo nickel and the Liberty Walking half dollar, a Lincoln cent or Jefferson nickel grading below PF-64 will have very limited appeal. The Mercury dime and Washington quarter, though scarcer than the last two, are likewise not very popular in grades under PF-64, though they still have value to collectors.

At the upper end of the grading scale, there are some budgetary limitations to consider. All of these early Proofs are scarce in grades above PF-66 and genuinely rare grading PF-68 or higher. Such pieces will bring very strong prices; a collector will want to research before determining his or her goal. A nicely matched Proof set of similar or very close grades will make for a much more appealing presentation than a set in which one or two coins are superb gems while the remaining pieces are of mediocre quality. It is best to determine one's upper grade limit for the most expensive coin in the set and make that the target grade for the entire set. Proof sets of matching or close grades are likewise easier to price and sell when that time ultimately comes. A further caveat is that as interest in extremely high-grade modern Proofs has been a focus mainly in the past several years, there are many coins being sent to the services for evaluation. It is expected that the populations of many coins will increase dramatically as more are certified. Still, a PF-68 will always command a higher market price than a PF-65 or PF-66.

Some of the flaws that often beset these older Proofs (and, to a lesser extent, those from later years) are hairline scratches, small spots known as "flyspecks," and irregular toning. Hairlines may be caused by movement within the cellophane sleeves in which the coins were delivered from the Mint, by careless insertion of the slides in a coin album, or by the rubbing action of a person wiping the coin after a chemical cleaning. The small black spots sometimes seen on Proof coins may be caused by human spittle (from talking over the coin without a mouth covering) or contamination by some organic matter such as skin flakes or paper particles. Toning can be either appealing or ugly, depending on the coloration and the pattern that results. Balanced toning of one or more colors can add tremendously to a coin's aesthetic value and is sometimes the result of decades' storage within coin albums. The blotchy, mottled toning often seen on Proofs from the 1936 to 1942 period comes from the cellophane sleeves in which the coins were delivered. When such toning is not desired, it may be removable by a professional numismatic conservator.

Historically, most collectors have preferred their Proof coins of 1936 and later years to be entirely untoned. Coins on which the natural toning actually adds to their value are rare for the 1936 to 1942 period and highly prized. Collectors are urged to be wary of pieces that have had their toning induced or accelerated through one or more processes. These are not desirable to a knowledgeable buyer, and the major grading services will reject them for certification in instances in which they can be identified.

Since cameo pieces (those having frosted lettering and devices) are extremely rare for 1936 to 1942 Proofs, only the most dedicated specialists will actively pursue them. The majority of Proof set collectors will never even see such coins, so they really play a very small role in the overall market.

The popular Lincoln cent merits some additional consideration on the part of Proof coin collectors, since the degree of surviving "mint red" (really *orange*, but popularly called red) color plays a strong role in determining its value. It should come as no surprise that Proof cents displaying all or nearly all of their original mint red (grading Proof RD) command the highest prices, but they may not always be the most attractive coins to the discriminating buyer. A red Proof cent that is free of spots and toning streaks is indeed a rare item and highly desirable, but most red cents do show some small black flyspecks. Collectors should be cautious of uncertified Proof cents that display blazing red color, as these may have been chemically cleaned. The best protection against such fraud is to buy only coins that have been certified by one of the major grading services.

For many collectors, a nice alternative to a fully red Proof cent is a coin grading Proof RB, or red and brown. Though fewer of these RB cents have been certified by the major grading services, they likely survive in greater numbers. Try to avoid coins that are bright red in one place and blotchy brown in another. The best example would be one whose red color has diminished uniformly throughout. If free of spots, streaks, and contact marks, such a coin may be very beautiful. The same applies to a Proof cent graded Proof BN, or brown. A brown Proof may still display amazing brilliance when turned under a light, and this protective layer of toning will reduce the likelihood of spotting and other atmospheric damage.

Included under the general category of cents grading PF BN are those that are neither red nor brown. Some absolutely amazing Proofs may be found that have naturally toned to varying shades of green or blue. In combination with a coin's original red color, such blue toning may result in a gorgeous magenta that many collectors find unbeatable for sheer eye appeal. Pricing such coins is an uncertain task, though several commercial price guides will include listings for the general categories of PF RB and PF BN.

Such intermediate color Proof cents may likewise be found for the issues dating 1950 and later, but the demand for these dates is restricted almost exclusively to those having full red color. The greater availability of these later dates in PF RD condition simply limits the market for coins having some other coloration. Certain of these color and toning concepts are difficult to explain in print and are best observed by viewing coins at a show or convention.

The Proof sets of 1950 to 1953 share many of the same flaws common to much of the surviving Proof coinage of earlier years. This is due to their similar packaging within cellophane. The switch to a softer plastic sleeve in 1954 and the superior flat packs in 1955 greatly reduced the incidences of hairline scratches. This resulted in slightly higher grades overall for the surviving population. The Proof coins of 1954 to 1964, as well as the Special Mint Sets of 1965 to 1967, typically are collected in grades PF-65 to PF-67. They remain fairly rare in higher grades, though certain issues within this span are exceptional in such regard.

Cameo pieces become collectible with the 1950 and later sets, though they remain a minority of each year's Proof mintage through 1964. A more detailed description of the relative rarity of cameo and deep cameo (or ultra cameo, as it is also called) coins may be found in the chapter that studies each Proof set by date.

Starting with the revived Proof coinage of 1968, the combination of high mintages, tighter quality control, and more protective packaging has resulted in a much greater survival rate in high grades. This trend accelerates with the Proof sets of 1978 and later, when the application of a cameo finish to the dies became quite consistent. From this point onward, gem Proofs are the rule rather than the exception, and Proofs of 1968 and later are seldom desired below PF-67. The typical Proof set of the 1980s onward will feature coins that are uniformly high in grade and deeply frosted on their lettering and devices.

PROOF SETS 1936–2005
A DATE-BY-DATE ANALYSIS

Understanding the Tables

Included for each Proof set is a table or tables listing each denomination within that particular set, as issued. These tables feature the combined totals of coins certified by the top three third-party grading services: ANACS; Professional Coin Grading Service (PCGS); and Numismatic Guaranty Corporation of America (NGC).

These figures are taken from the October 2004 edition of the *PCGS Population Report*, the October 2004 edition of the *NGC Census Report*, and *ANACS Population Report* data from early 2005.

Also found within these tables are average values for complete sets of certified Proof coins at various levels (PF-65, PF-66, etc.). Proof coin expert Rick Tomaska generously provided this information, while additional pricing information was supplied by valuations editor Lawrence Stack. Kenneth Bressett and his team of Red Book pricing contributors assisted with the valuation of uncertified sets.

It should be noted that these values are simply a guide to current market conditions, which may vary as additional coins are certified, and as demand increases or decreases for a particular set. Actual sales prices may be different from one dealer to the next, depending on the dealer's current inventory and need, if any, for additional sets.

The uncertified values that appear below the tables are for sets of average quality. Average quality may be defined as:

- PF-64 for sets dated 1936–1942
- PF-65 for sets dated 1950–1953
- PF-66 for sets dated 1954–1967
- PF-67 for sets dated 1968–1977
- PF-68 for sets dated 1978–1988
- PF-69 for all sets dated 1989 and later.

In some instances, the uncertified values may be slightly higher than those of lower certified grades. This is because uncertified Proof sets in their original packaging are presumed by the hobby to average a particular grade, this grade varying with the age of the set. For most sets dated 1965 and later, the certified values are significantly higher than for uncertified coins. This discrepancy is due to both the low market value of Proof sets from these years and the expense of having these lower-value coins certified.

VINTAGE PROOF SETS
1936-1942

1936

Coins shown at 90% actual size

Coins shown at 90% actual size

3,837 Complete Sets Possible

Denomination	PF-64		PF-65	
	Cert. Population	Value	Cert. Population	Value
Cent, Satin (Red)	74		55	
Cent, Brilliant (Red)	414		154	
Nickel, Satin	156		238	
Nickel, Brilliant	223		328	
Dime	643		577	
Quarter	643		378	
Half Dollar	855		713	
Complete Set, Satin Cent and Nickel		$7,000		$13,000
Complete Set, Brilliant Cent and Nickel		$9,000		$13,500

Original Price: $1.81 for all five denominations, though each piece could be purchased separately. Proof cents were priced at 16¢, nickels and dimes at 20¢, quarters at 50¢ and halves at 75¢. A charge of 8¢ for postage was applied to all mail orders, thus arriving at the total of $1.89 for a complete set when ordered by mail. Single coin purchases were each charged the same 8¢ postage, so it was clearly to one's advantage to buy a complete set.

Uncertified Value: $7,000

Original Packaging: Each coin was placed into a transparent cellophane envelope just slightly wider than the coin itself. For orders of multiple coins or complete sets, these envelopes were stapled together at one corner. The stapled envelopes were wrapped in tissue paper for protection and sealed inside small cardboard boxes.

A variety of different boxes was used for mail orders, each box being selected to fit the size of the order. Thus, there was no standard size, and the boxes featured no printed text or logos. While primitive and lacking any sense of presentation, this simple packaging kept the issue price of Proof sets quite low for many years. It remained the U.S. Mint's method of shipping Proof coins through mid-1955, though a standardized, square box was introduced beginning with the 1950 sets. Considered simply a means of delivery for coins that would ultimately be placed into albums or commercially produced plastic holders, surviving examples of this original packaging are very rare and have some collectible value in their own right.

Commentary: The sale of Proof coins to the public resumed April 28, 1936, after a hiatus of some twenty years. This move was prompted by growing complaints from collectors about the unavailability of such pieces. The Mint's position had been that the concave fields of the current issues precluded the kind of die polishing that was used with Proof coins of older types, which had flat, brilliant fields and frosted lettering and devices. While this was true, a new method would have to be devised that accommodated the current coinage.

A resumption of the Matte proofing technique used by the U.S. Mint from 1908 to 1916 was out of the question, as collectors had voted against it with annually declining sales. In fact, these poor results, along with the introduction of bold new designs for the silver coinage in 1916, are what prompted a discontinuance of Proof coinage that year.

The first deliveries of Proofs in 1936 included coins that, while clearly different from regular circulating pieces, were not quite what collectors anticipated. The cents and nickels in particular were only semi-brilliant and may be more accurately described as having a satin finish. Indeed, this is how they are labeled by the major grading services. Coins certified some years ago may still carry the designations "Type 1" and "Type 2," but it is now clearly understood that the differences between satin Proofs and brilliant Proofs represent not a change in type, but only in die preparation.

Responding to complaints from purchasers, the Mint went back to the drawing board and began producing Proofs that were fully brilliant throughout. These are comparable to the Proof coins of 1937 and later years, and they are by far more popular with collectors. Ironically, the Satin Finish Proofs are more rare, but this has little impact on their desirability, and for this reason their market value is smaller.

While there exist differences in brilliance for all five denominations, it is only the cents and nickels that are distinctive enough to be labeled accordingly. The greater natural brilliance of silver as a metal makes the early Proof dimes, quarters, and halves of 1936 fairly similar to the ones made later in the year. Cameo Proofs—those having some frosting on the raised devices—are extremely rare.

The quality of surviving pieces varies tremendously. The cents in particular have suffered over time, most showing flaws such as toning streaks, fingerprints, and small black spots commonly called flyspecks. This spotting is also evident on other denominations, but it is especially troubling with the highly reactive composition of the cent.

The original packaging for the Proof coins of 1936 to 1942 contributed to these problems in two ways. First, its simplicity and unattractiveness prompted collectors to remove the coins and place them in albums, where the sulfurous cardboard and paper dust reacted with them. Second, the cellophane's own composition caused coins left in it to develop a milky, tan-colored film that cannot be safely removed except by professional conservators. Over the years, many collectors and dealers have attempted to restore early Proof coins themselves, with mostly unfortunate results.

There is anecdotal evidence that Proofs of the 1936 to 1942 period purchased in person at the Philadelphia Mint were not distributed in cellophane, which was seemingly reserved for mail orders. Proofs acquired in person were reportedly presented in small tissues that were simply folded over. This was the usual practice in earlier years to 1916, but no surviving examples of such tissues are reported.

Perhaps due to the initial complaints about quality, sales of Proof coins in 1936 were quite low by later standards. These pieces are all quite scarce, regardless of condition, and the 1936 Proof set is easily the most valuable and desired set in this long series.

1937

Coins shown at 90% actual size

Vintage Proof Sets

Coins shown at 90% actual size

5,542 Complete Sets Possible

Denomination	PF-64		PF-65	
	Cert. Population	Value	Cert. Population	Value
Cent (Red)	622		456	
Nickel	532		880	
Dime	573		750	
Quarter	480		642	
Half Dollar	866		848	
Complete Set		$3,500		$4,500

Original Price: $1.81 for a complete set. Single Proofs of any denomination could be purchased at the following prices: cents, 16¢; nickels and dimes, 20¢; quarters, 50¢; halves, 75¢. A charge of 8¢ postage was applied to all mail orders.

Uncertified Value: $4,000

Original Packaging: Each coin was placed into a transparent cellophane envelope just slightly wider than the coin itself. For orders of multiple coins or complete sets, these envelopes were stapled together at one corner. The stapled envelopes were wrapped in tissue paper for some measure of protection and sealed inside small cardboard boxes.

Commentary: The Philadelphia Mint had more or less perfected its proofing process, and 1937 Proof coins are of fairly consistent finish and quality. All have the fully brilliant style of later 1936 Proofs. A precious few are known with cameo contrast on one side, and even more rarely on both sides.

The Proof cents of 1937 are very difficult to locate without spotting and staining. Some have mellowed in color and can no longer be certified as Proof Red, yet there are many examples in Red-Brown and Brown that remain quite attractive. Coins that have been stored in albums for many years will sometimes display vibrant, multi-color toning that is quite appealing. Such coins will be certified as PF BN, though that scarcely gives a true picture of their appearance. While toning is very desirable to the advanced collector, the Proof coins most hobbyists still prefer are fully red.

As the final year that Buffalo nickels were coined in Proof, this date should have realized an upward spike in sales. Unfortunately for collectors, the Treasury Department did not announce the demise of this popular coin type until the following spring, and sales of 1937 Proofs had already ended. This left a total of little more than ten thousand Proof Buffalo nickels available to collectors, not including the Matte Proof issues of 1913 to 1916. As a type, it is thus the rarest of these early Proofs and highly desired.

As would prove the case almost every year that Proof coins could be purchased singly, the quarter dollar had the lowest mintage of the five denominations. A coin of very recent design, and one that was not particularly liked by collectors of the time, it received the least interest from buyers. It is likely that few quarters were purchased separately and that most demand resulted from collectors purchasing complete sets. Though it is the key coin in terms of mintage, this fact is not reflected in its current value.

1938

Coins shown at 90% actual size

Coins shown at 90% actual size

8,045 Complete Sets Possible

Denomination	PF-64		PF-65	
	Cert. Population	Value	Cert. Population	Value
Cent (Red)	661		647	
Nickel	498		850	
Dime	768		1,211	
Quarter	642		842	
Half Dollar	843		1,059	
Complete Set		$1,900		$2,300

Original Price: $1.81 for a complete set. Single Proofs of any denomination could be purchased at the following prices: cents, 16¢; nickels and dimes, 20¢; quarters, 50¢; halves, 75¢. A charge of 8¢ postage was applied to all mail orders.

Uncertified Value: $1,900

Original Packaging: Each coin was placed into a transparent cellophane envelope just slightly wider than the coin itself. For orders of multiple coins or complete sets, these envelopes were stapled together at one corner. The stapled envelopes were wrapped in tissue paper for some measure of protection and sealed inside small cardboard boxes.

Commentary: The big news for 1938 was the debut of the Jefferson nickel. While today's collectors regret that the popular Indian Head/Buffalo type was not continued for a few more years, hobbyists of 1938 eagerly anticipated the new issue. Unfortunately, these coins were not ready until the fall. Most collectors went ahead and ordered the other denominations early in the year, because the Mint still permitted Proofs to be ordered in any combination desired.

As may be seen from the published mintage figures, the new nickel was a runaway bestseller. Because the number of other Proofs sold in 1938 was up significantly from the year before, it is quite possible that some collectors went ahead and ordered complete Proof sets, including the nickel, after having already purchased the other coins earlier in the year.

Beginning with this year, the number of Proofs surviving in gem condition likewise increase. There was a growing demand for the Proof coins of 1936 and 1937 among those who had been caught napping or who were just discovering the hobby, and the prices of these issues were already above their original cost. This proved to be just a precursor of what was to come, as the 1936 set in particular caused a speculative mania.

1938 Proofs showing any degree of cameo contrast are very rare and highly desired by collectors.

Collector's Notebook – 1938
Buffalo nickel reverse

Although 1938 was the final year of the Indian Head (or Buffalo) nickel, the last Proofs of the series were struck in 1937. Historians might never agree on the identity of the model for the "Indian Head" portrait, though many contend that designer James E. Fraser fashioned the work after three different Native Americans. One thing is certain: this classic coin, with its symbolism of the American West, ranks as one of the nation's most popular.

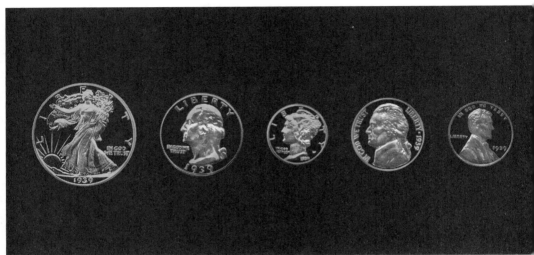

Coins shown at 90% actual size

Coins shown at 90% actual size

8,795 Complete Sets Possible

Denomination	PF-64		PF-65	
	Cert. Population	Value	Cert. Population	Value
Cent (Red)	606		658	
Nickel	311		613	
Dime	473		1,057	
Quarter	471		794	
Half Dollar	769		1,073	
Complete Set		$1,800		$2,200

Original Price: $1.81 for a complete set. Single Proofs of any denomination could be purchased at the following prices: cents, 16¢; nickels and dimes, 20¢; quarters, 50¢; halves, 75¢. A charge of 8¢ postage was applied to all mail orders.

Uncertified Value: $1,800

Original Packaging: Each coin was placed into a transparent cellophane envelope just slightly wider than the coin itself. For orders of multiple coins or complete sets, these envelopes were stapled together at one corner. The stapled envelopes were wrapped in tissue paper for some measure of protection and sealed inside small cardboard boxes.

Commentary: By 1939, the cent and the nickel were in a race to see which coin was most popular with collectors. It is hard to imagine a time when the Jefferson nickel was a source of excitement, yet this type remained fairly scarce in circulation until 1940. The nation's depression-wracked economy slowed the release of new coins, and Jeffersons were still a rare novelty in 1939. This undoubtedly led to the strong sales of Proof nickels for this date.

The 1939 Proof nickel is of interest to variety collectors, as it comes with two distinctive reverses. The original Jefferson nickel reverse of 1938 featured wavy and somewhat incomplete steps on Jefferson's home, Monticello. The Mint's engraving staff sharpened these steps sometime during 1939 by preparing an entirely new master hub, and both varieties may be found for Proofs and circulation pieces alike. Proofs having the sharpened steps, a variety known as the Reverse of 1940, are noticeably scarcer than those with the earlier reverse, and command a premium price.

Proofs of this date having some cameo contrast are rare, yet they seem to exist for all five denominations. This is more likely to be found on the silver issues, as the greater natural brilliance of silver provides for more noticeable contrast.

Collector's Notebook – 1939
Jefferson nickel obverse

The first year of the new Jefferson nickel—1938—saw the modest mintage of about 30 million coins total, struck for circulation at the Philadelphia, Denver, and San Francisco mints. In 1939 that quantity skyrocketed to more than 130 million. Proof mintages remained small, however, and didn't break the 100,000 mark until 1953.

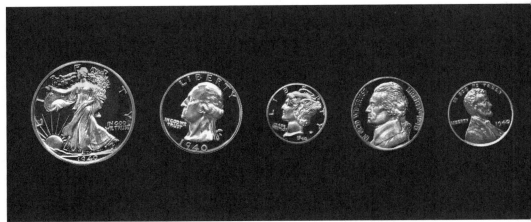

Coins shown at 90% actual size

Coins shown at 90% actual size

11,246 Complete Sets Possible

Denomination	PF-64		PF-65	
	Cert. Population	Value	Cert. Population	Value
Cent (Red)	589		676	
Nickel	259		561	
Dime	769		1,346	
Quarter	554		953	
Half Dollar	963		1,408	
Complete Set		$1,500		$2,000

Original Price: $1.81 for a complete set. Single Proofs of any denomination could be purchased at the following prices: cents, 16¢; nickels and dimes, 20¢; quarters, 50¢; halves, 75¢. A charge of 8¢ postage was applied to all mail orders.

Uncertified Value: $1,500

Original Packaging: Each coin was placed into a transparent cellophane envelope just slightly wider than the coin itself. For orders of multiple coins or complete sets, these envelopes were stapled together at one corner. The stapled envelopes were wrapped in tissue paper for some measure of protection and sealed inside small cardboard boxes.

Commentary: Collectors were keenly aware of the aftermarket price increases for the Proof sets of 1936, and sales of Proof coins in 1940 showed a notable increase from the year before. Prosperity was returning to the United States after a decade of economic depression, and this undoubtedly encouraged sales, too.

Once again, the quarter dollar registered the lowest sales, though time has rendered these slight differences meaningless. Most of the 1936 to 1942 Proofs have long since been removed from their original envelopes, so their subsequent handling weighs more heavily on their survival rate than does the respective numbers coined.

Like the nickels of 1939, those dated 1940 are transitional. The majority feature the sharper steps of Monticello introduced in 1939, yet a few were coined with older dies that were impressed from the old hub having the wavy steps typical of 1938 nickels and most of the 1939 nickels. Collectors eagerly seek the 1938 Reverse nickel among the 1940 Proofs.

The Mint's achieving of a fully brilliant finish after 1936 often came at a price in terms of design detail. Its die polishing was very harsh, and this tended to soften some of the details rather than enhance them. In addition, the dies wore quickly, and this further eroded some details. Wear was evident as shallow flow lines radiating outward from the center of the die. These lines were transferred to the coins struck from such dies, a phenomenon that a later generation of Mint employees described as "starburst."

Instead of quickly retiring Proof dies as they became worn, Mint personnel repolished them to a full brilliance. This further eroded the details, and it even wiped out some shallow features altogether. An example is the lapel of Lincoln's coat on the cent. Where it meets the coin's field, this feature is in very low relief, and repeated polishing of the dies removed enough metal to diminish it significantly. Another example of overzealous polishing of the dies is seen on the Mercury dime, where the band that secures the rods of the fasces is left hanging at the bottom. Being a fairly shallow feature, one that is near the coin's border, it was particularly vulnerable to abrasive polishing of the die. On this and other dates of Proof dimes, it may appear very thin or even partially obliterated.

1941

Coins shown at 90% actual size

Coins shown at 90% actual size

15,287 Complete Sets Possible

Denomination	PF-64		PF-65	
	Cert. Population	Value	Cert. Population	Value
Cent (Red)	716		597	
Nickel	329		758	
Dime	1,216		18,521,895	
Quarter	681		1,199	
Half Dollar	1,505		1,956	
Complete Set		$1,500		$1,800

Original Price: $1.81 for a complete set. Single Proofs of any denomination could be purchased at the following prices: cents, 16¢; nickels and dimes, 20¢; quarters, 50¢; halves, 75¢. A charge of 8¢ postage was applied to all mail orders.

Uncertified Value: $1,500

Original Packaging: Each coin was placed into a transparent cellophane envelope just slightly wider than the coin itself. For orders of multiple coins or complete sets, these envelopes were stapled together at one corner. The stapled envelopes were wrapped in tissue paper for some measure of protection and sealed inside small cardboard boxes.

Commentary: Proof mintages rose again this year, with the quarter dollar still lagging a bit. As mintages rose, so did the number of dies used. This created a greater possibility of cameo Proofs, because such frosting appeared in the devices only when the dies were fresh. Even so, cameo pieces are rare for this date, as they are for all Proofs of 1936 to 1942.

The Proofs made in 1941 are slightly better than those of earlier years in at least one respect: the excessive die polishing that obliterated some of the more shallow design elements on earlier Proofs was not as evident this year. One particularly glaring exception is the 1941 half dollar die lacking the artist's monogrammed initials, AW. This feature normally appears near the border at about four to five o'clock on the reverse, yet many of the Proof halves of this date are lacking the monogram entirely. It was polished right off the die, along with a number of other design elements that were either removed or greatly diminished. While some collectors seek this variety, it is really just a late state of the die and quite common. The discriminating hobbyist should attempt to find a sharp impression with all details complete.

Collector's Notebook – 1941
Liberty Walking half dollar, obverse

The first mintage of Proof Liberty Walking half dollars was struck in 1936—a quantity of fewer than 4,000 pieces. Proof quantities climbed steadily through the 1930s and early '40s, culminating with just over 21,000 pieces in 1942. In 1941, the year the Empire of Japan bombed Pearl Harbor, 15,412 Proofs were struck. By 1943, the United States was embroiled in battle, and Proof coins took a back seat to the war effort. No more would be minted until 1950.

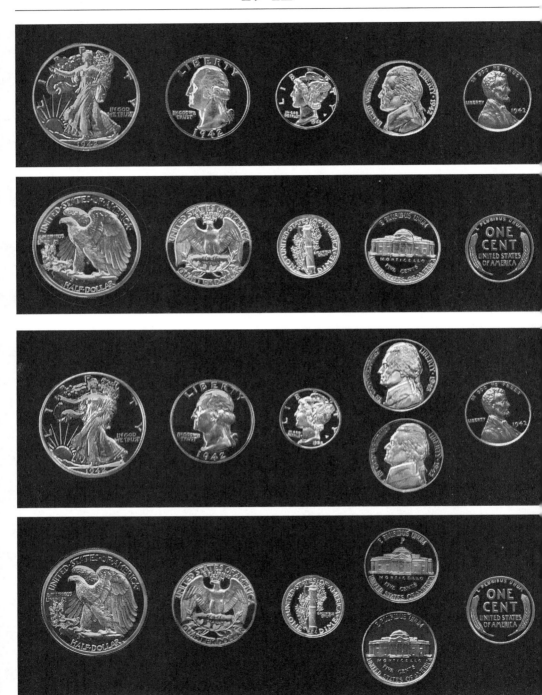

Coins shown at 90% actual size

21,120 Complete Sets Possible

Denomination	PF-64		PF-65	
	Cert. Population	Value	Cert. Population	Value
Cent (Red)	1,146		592	
Nickel, Regular Alloy	362		1,204	
Nickel, Silver Alloy	941		1,778	
Dime	1,585		2,465	
Quarter	1,007		1,656	
Half Dollar	3,459		2,310	
Complete Set, One Nickel		$1,700		$1,900
Complete Set, Two Nickels		$1,900		$2,150

Original Price: $1.81 for a complete set. Single Proofs of any denomination could be purchased at the following prices: cents, 16¢; nickels and dimes, 20¢; quarters, 50¢; halves, 75¢. A charge of 8¢ postage was applied to all mail orders.

The copper-silver-manganese nickels were not available until the fall, long after most collectors had purchased their Proof sets for the year, so these were sold mostly as singles at 28¢, including postage.

Uncertified Value: $1,325 (with one nickel); $1,425 (with both nickels)

Original Packaging: Each coin was placed into a transparent cellophane envelope just slightly wider than the coin itself. For orders of multiple coins or complete sets, these envelopes were stapled together at one corner. The stapled envelopes were wrapped in tissue paper for some measure of protection and sealed inside small cardboard boxes.

Commentary: The 1942 Proof set has long been a favorite for several reasons, the most obvious being that it includes six coins instead of five.

As it was not known at the beginning of 1942 that a change in the nickel's composition would occur, the Mint went about its normal offering of Proof coins. It is likely that initial sales were only moderately higher than in 1941, but the introduction of a second nickel in the fall evidently prompted at least some collectors to order complete duplicate sets. The quantities sold of all five denominations are higher than would be expected, though the nickel clearly became that year's favorite.

The change in alloy for the five-cent piece was authorized by law on October 8, 1942. The regular composition of 75% copper and 25% nickel was replaced with one of 56% copper, 35% silver, and 9% manganese. While the stated purpose was to save nickel (for the manufacture of armor plating and other war-related products), this change offered the benefit of reducing the coin's copper content as well. Copper's importance to the war effort was further indicated by its elimination from the cent in 1943, as well (sadly, no Proofs were coined in 1943 to provide collectors with an example of that ill-fated coin).

Both editions of the five-cent piece enjoyed very large mintages for the time period, and neither is rare today except in the highest grades. Collectors, who often include them as stand-alone items within their type sets, favor the wartime "nickels."

Another feature that makes the 1942 Proof set a very desirable one is that its quality is generally the highest of the 1936 to 1942 period. The Mint became increasingly skilled at polishing the dies, and this was nearly perfected by 1942. While some Proofs are found that were produced from severely polished dies, most coins of this date are more sharply struck and richly detailed than earlier pieces.

One curiosity is that the Proof cent of this year is quite challenging to locate in fully red condition. No definitive explanation for this scarcity is known. Tin was eliminated from the cent's alloy midway through the year, because the war had cut off America's supply of this metal, but that should not have had any visible effect.

On the positive side, cameo Proofs are somewhat more available for this date than for all others of 1936 to 1941, though they still form a very small minority of the surviving Proofs.

1950

Coins shown at 90% actual size

Coins shown at 90% actual size

51,386 Complete Sets Possible

Denomination	PF-65		PF-65 Cameo		PF-65 Ultra Cameo		PF-66		PF-66 Cameo		PF-66 Ultra Cameo	
	Pop.	Value	Pop.	Value	Pop.	Value	Pop.	Value	Pop.	Value	Pop.	Value
Cent (Red)	523		139		28		336		97		15	
Nickel	347		45		2		623		115		8	
Dime	349		25		2		623		84		4	
Quarter	694		55		4		687		71		4	
Half Dollar	1,376		190		9		649		58		3	
Complete Set		$675		$1,500		$10,000		$725		$7,000		$10,000

Original Price: $2.10 for all five denominations, sold only in complete sets.

Uncertified Value: $700

Original Packaging: Each coin was placed into a transparent cellophane envelope just slightly wider than the coin itself. As only complete sets could be ordered beginning in 1950, all five envelopes were stapled together at one corner. The stapled envelopes were wrapped in tissue paper for some measure of protection and sealed inside small square, gray cardboard boxes. Depending on the environment in which they were stored, some of these boxed sets may reveal rust on the staples. While this was not a direct hazard to the coins within, it suggests that the coins were exposed to moisture, which tended to result in spotting.

In contrast to Proof set deliveries of 1936 to 1942, a standard-size box was adopted beginning in 1950. This was dictated by the fact that only complete sets were being offered, and it permitted the sets to be boxed in advance of actual orders. Measuring approximately $2\frac{3}{8}$ inches square by $\frac{7}{8}$ inches deep, each box was sealed with a single strip of postal tape wrapped around it. From 1950 through 1954, these boxes were not labeled, though most seen have the date written atop in pencil. It is not certain whether this was done at the Mint or by owners of the sets.

An appropriately sized shipping box was selected to protect the boxed sets. While collectors desire the individual set boxes, a fair number having survived, the outer mailers mostly have been discarded and are seldom sought by collectors.

Commentary: The strain of producing a tremendous numbers of coins for circulation during the World War II years led to a suspension of Proof coin manufacture after 1942. As soon as the war ended, collectors began to plead for its resumption, but a spokesperson for the U.S. Mint claimed that the department was struggling with budget restraints imposed by the post-war recession and accumulated Federal debt. A bill to provide the funding for resumption of Proof production was not passed until 1950, being signed into law by President Harry S Truman on May 10.

Orders were accepted beginning July 17, by which time 10,000 sets had already been produced. The coin collecting hobby had experienced marked growth since 1942, and total sales of Proof sets were double those of the last pre-war issue. The popularity of this year's set was undoubtedly increased by the fact that it included the first Proofs made for both the Roosevelt dime and Franklin half dollar.

The Mint had to once again relearn the art of polishing Proof dies and planchets. Many of the 1950 Proof coins have a finish more satiny than brilliant, much like the early sets of 1936. While the Satin Finish Proofs have a certain unique charm, collectors clearly prefer brilliant fields. When such coins also possess frosty white lettering and devices, for the all-too-rare cameo quality, they are better still.

Cameo Proofs, while available for all denominations of 1950, are very scarce. Deep or ultra cameo pieces are extremely rare and may be expected to bring substantial premiums.

The Proof coins of 1950 are very scarce in grades exceeding PF-65. The harshness of the cellophane envelopes, combined with the coins' freedom to slide around within them, led to some pieces acquiring hairline scratches that diminish their grades. Many of the Proofs produced before the 1955 introduction of pliofilm packaging suffer from such hairlines, as well as cloudy toning. Collectors' inexpert attempts at cleaning these coins often led to further and much more severe hairlining.

Coins shown at 90% actual size

Coins shown at 90% actual size

57,500 Complete Sets Possible

Denomination	PF-65		PF-65 Cameo		PF-65 Ultra Cameo		PF-66		PF-66 Cameo		PF-66 Ultra Cameo	
	Pop.	Value	Pop.	Value	Pop.	Value	Pop.	Value	Pop.	Value	Pop.	Value
Cent (Red)	349		29		0		355		42		0	
Nickel	256		29		0		586		129		3	
Dime	245		19		1		566		107		4	
Quarter	476		45		25		533		86		5	
Half Dollar	1,184		190		25		675		126		22	
Complete Set		$600		$1,000		$3,000		$700		$4,300		$9,000

Original Price: $2.10

Uncertified Value: $650

Original Packaging: Each coin was placed into a transparent cellophane envelope just slightly wider than the coin itself, and all five envelopes were stapled together at one corner. The stapled envelopes were wrapped in tissue paper for some measure of protection and sealed inside small cardboard boxes with postal tape.

Commentary: The Proofs of 1951, like those of 1950, come in two finishes. While most are fully brilliant, a certain percentage may be found having partially brilliant or somewhat satiny fields. It is likely that such coins resulted from incomplete polishing of the dies. While not as popular, they do tend to reveal more detail of the coins' designs, since the more aggressively polished dies sometimes had their low-relief elements polished away completely.

Cameo Proofs are rare, but they are known for each denomination. Deep or ultra cameo pieces are very rare. There is some anecdotal evidence that collectors of the time took notice of such distinctions, though there appears to have been no premium attached to them until the 1970s. Some veteran collectors would have made a comparison between modern Proofs and those of the pre-1916 period and realized that modern cameo pieces were exceptional and worthy of some interest.

Though most of the Proof cents coined since 1950 retain much of their mint red color, there still exists a market for Proofs certified as Red-Brown, or RB in grading service shorthand. Cameo pieces are rare enough that they carry a premium even when not fully red. This is certainly true of Proof cents through at least 1970, though for subsequent years anything less than full red is not very desirable.

Two collectible varieties are known for the Proofs of 1951. A small number of cent Proofs may be found with die doubling in the motto IN GOD WE TRUST. A rare variety of the Proof nickel features die doubling in Jefferson's profile and in the word TRUST.

Collector's Notebook – 1951

Washington quarter, reverse

In 1951, Proof mintages of the silver Washington quarter dollar were in their relative infancy, with fewer than 60,000 struck. Like the population of post-war baby boomers, though, those numbers would grow throughout the 1950s—breaking the million-coin mark in 1957, and again in 1959. From there the Proofs grew to maturity, until close to four million were struck in 1964, the final year of the 90% silver quarter.

1952

Coins shown at 90% actual size

Coins shown at 90% actual size

81,980 Complete Sets Possible

Denomination	PF-65		PF-65 Cameo		PF-65 Ultra Cameo		PF-66		PF-66 Cameo		PF-66 Ultra Cameo	
	Pop.	Value	Pop.	Value	Pop.	Value	Pop.	Value	Pop.	Value	Pop.	Value
Cent (Red)	313		220		3		347		47		1	
Nickel	217		12		1		563		784		5	
Dime	223		8		1		530		45		0	
Quarter	424		32		3		647		85		9	
Half Dollar	1,344		232		10		873		238		7	
Complete Set		$375		$1,000		$6,000		$750		$3,100		$7,000

Original Price: $2.10

Uncertified Value: $350

Original Packaging: Each coin was placed into a transparent cellophane envelope just slightly wider than the coin itself, and all five envelopes were stapled together at one corner. The stapled envelopes were wrapped in tissue paper for some measure of protection and sealed inside small cardboard boxes with postal tape.

Commentary: From 1936 through the early 1970s, the normal finish for United States Proof coins is uniformly brilliant in fields and devices. Still, some coins may reveal the onset of satiny fields as a result of losing their polish. These coins have fine lines radiating from their centers toward their borders, a condition a later generation of Mint employees would describe as "starburst." When these lines were discovered on a die's face, the die would be removed from the press and repolished to a full brilliance. Though this removed some of the shallower details from the die, it did give the effect that collectors expected. Repeated polishing of the dies, with resulting loss of detail, was all too typical of Proofs dated 1936 to 1964.

One interesting variety found for 1952 is the so-called "Superbird" quarter. Proof dies were frequently cleaned after every couple dozen or so strikes, using alcohol and a soft cloth. Occasionally, a fiber from these cloths would remain on the die face or in one of its cavities, and an impression of this slim thread would be transferred to the coin and die at the moment of striking. One such instance is found on some of the 1952 Proof quarters. What makes this occurrence stand out from the many others is that the fiber left a raised impression at the very center of the eagle's breast on each coin struck from that reverse die. The short impression is curled into the shape of the letter S, and this evokes an image of Superman's costume, with its bold S on his chest. A popular and highly sought variety, this is just one of the many fun oddities associated with our Proof coinage.

Cameo Proofs of this date are quite scarce, with deep cameo pieces being genuinely rare. While these premium coins are most desired in high grades, even lesser specimens will bring good prices for their distinctive finish. Not being fully appreciated at the time, cameo Proofs were subject to the same mishandling and poor storage suffered by many ordinary Proofs produced before the Mint adopted hard plastic holders in 1966.

The idea for such holders may have resulted in part from initiative shown by the private sector. The marketing of rigid, screw-together holders of acrylic plastic began in 1945, and these holders became the item of choice for housing complete Proof sets during the 1950s and '60s. Introduced just a few years later were snap-together holders made from polystyrene. While not as attractive, and offering less protection from abrasion, the styrene holders were also less expensive than acrylics.

Coins shown at 90% actual size

Coins shown at 90% actual size

128,800 Complete Sets Possible

Denomination	PF-65		PF-65 Cameo		PF-65 Ultra Cameo		PF-66		PF-66 Cameo		PF-66 Ultra Cameo	
	Pop.	Value	Pop.	Value	Pop.	Value	Pop.	Value	Pop.	Value	Pop.	Value
Cent	297		54		6		392		74		10	
Nickel	162		6		1		469		41		0	
Dime	242		15		13		438		79		29	
Quarter	371		342		7		1,041		182		15	
Half Dollar	1,391		380		16		1,013		416		30	
Complete Set		$350		$850		$2,200		$475		$850		$3,500

Original Price: $2.10

Uncertified Value: $310

Original Packaging: Each coin was placed into a transparent cellophane envelope just slightly wider than the coin itself, and all five envelopes were stapled together at one corner. The stapled envelopes were wrapped in tissue paper for some measure of protection and sealed inside small cardboard boxes with postal tape.

Commentary: 1953 was the year that Proof set sales really took off, as a speculative market grew in the 1936 to 1942 sets and even the 1950 to 1952 sets. Already the 51,386 sets sold in 1950 made this date a modern rarity, at least in relative terms.

Despite a larger mintage, the Proof coins of 1953 are scarce as cameo pieces and very rare with deep or ultra cameo frosting. As with most Proofs from the 1950s and '60s, it is the half dollar that is most in demand in gem cameo or deep cameo condition. Being the largest and heaviest coin in the set, it is the one most subject to suffering hairline scratches and abrasions. Proof quarters, once largely neglected, have recently become quite popular as a consequence of the state quarters program, which has increased interest in the Washington series across the board.

Cameo Proofs are certainly more readily available for coins dated 1950 and later than they are for the 1936 to 1942 issues, though they remain in the minority of Proof pieces minted through the early 1970s. During this period, the Mint took no special effort to preserve the frosty texture that the dies possessed when first placed into the coin press. Some 3,000 to 5,000 Proofs may have been made from each die before it was retired from Proof production, and this frost was quickly worn smooth through repeated striking of coins. Only the first few hundred Proofs from each die could be expected to show any frostiness. Perhaps only the first few dozen impressions would result in coins having deep or ultra cameo contrast, and these are consistently the most desired of Proofs among specialists.

Collectible varieties for 1953 include a doubled-die obverse cent with doubling quite visible in numerals "19" of the date. While not especially rare, this one is very popular. Somewhat scarcer, though still obtainable for any interested collector, is the 1953 nickel with die doubling in the motto IN GOD WE TRUST. This doubling is slight, and it will require a magnifying glass to see. A truly fascinating variety is the tripled-die obverse 1953 Proof quarter. It shows faint extra outlines to both sides of the date numerals.

Coins shown at 90% actual size

Coins shown at 90% actual size

233,300 Complete Sets Possible

Denomination	PF-66		PF-66 Cameo		PF-66 Ultra Cameo	
	Cert. Population	Value	Cert. Population	Value	Cert. Population	Value
Cent (Red)	369		115		11	
Nickel	386		71		5	
Dime	409		81		2	
Quarter	655		219		19	
Half Dollar	1,523		554		44	
Complete Set		$235		$450		$2,200

Original Price: $2.10

Uncertified Value: $175

Original Packaging: For some of the 1954 sets, each coin was placed into a transparent cellophane or envelope just slightly wider than the coin itself, and all five envelopes were stapled together at one end. An alternative packaging introduced during the course of this year's deliveries replaced the cellophane envelopes used since 1936 with ones of softer polyethylene, as cellophane tends to become brittle over time. This was done evidently in response to complaints from collectors that the cellophane envelopes were subject to splitting, while their harshness sometimes led to the formation of hairline scratches on the Proof coins' delicate surfaces. The new envelopes were similar to the ones still produced commercially for the hobby and commonly called "polybags."

Whichever material was used, the stapled envelopes were wrapped in tissue paper for some measure of protection and sealed inside small cardboard boxes with postal tape.

Commentary: Sales of Proof sets nearly doubled from 1953, and the Proofs of this date are indeed much more readily available than those of earlier years.

The change in packaging did cut down a bit on the tendency of Proof coins to suffer faint hairlines, but it also created a new problem. Proofs of this date stored in their original polyethylene envelopes, as well as 1955 Proofs in similar packaging, often show deep and unattractive toning. The combination of this plastic and the cardboard box could result in a somewhat purplish cast to the coins. Professional conservation is recommended for such pieces. Over the years, many have already been cleaned by their owners with mixed results.

The cents coined for circulation at the Philadelphia Mint in 1954 were often a bit dark, as made, but this doesn't seem to have affected the Proof cents. Gem examples of all five denominations, while certainly not common, are available to collectors willing to pay market value. Cameo examples are somewhat more readily available for this date than for earlier ones, as the greater mintage prompted the use of more dies than previously. Because each die had a deep cameo finish when placed in the press for the first time, this created a greater pool of desirable Proofs. As always for pre-1970s Proofs, deep cameo examples remain rare.

378,200 Complete Sets Possible

Denomination	PF-66		PF-66 Cameo		PF-66 Ultra Cameo	
	Cert. Population	Value	Cert. Population	Value	Cert. Population	Value
Cent (Red)	387		113		19	
Nickel	74		80		7	
Dime	344		83		7	
Quarter	521		145		43	
Half Dollar	2,039		578		58	
Complete Set		$205		$375		$2,000

Original Price: $2.10

Uncertified Value: $150 (individual envelopes); $175 included above (pliofilm package)

Original Packaging: The 1955 sets were delivered with two highly distinctive types of packaging. Early orders were packaged in the traditional individual envelopes, as described for the 1954 sets. Most seen included polyethylene envelopes, though there are reports of the older style cellophane being used. In either instance, the stapled envelopes were wrapped in tissue paper for some measure of protection and sealed inside small cardboard boxes with postal tape. Across this tape, on the top of the box was rubber-stamped 1955 *UNITED STATES PROOF COINS*.

Midway through 1955, the U.S. Mint adopted a more sophisticated method of packaging and delivering Proof sets. The five coins were sealed into a single, soft plastic envelope with pockets for each coin, these being arranged in two rows. The coins were permitted to slide about within their respective pockets, but they could not come into contact with one another. A sixth pocket held an embossed seal made of paper and having a metallic finish. This was octagonal in shape and featured US MINT PHILADELPHIA printed in blue on silver.

The Mint described its new plastic envelope as "pliofilm," though it appears to be some form of polyethylene. Each set was protected from damage by two strips of cardstock, and all three pieces were inserted, along with a brief fact sheet, into a buff-colored mailing envelope. This envelope carried a pre-printed return address for the Philadelphia Mint and a discreet notation of its contents. Though the recipient's address could be typed or written directly on this envelope, most customers ordered multiple sets, so a shipping box of corresponding size was used. This form of packaging remained in use through the Special Mint Set of 1965.

Commentary: Sales of Proof sets rose dramatically again this year, with the total exceeding that of 1954 by more than 50%. Speculation in Proof sets was growing, with most collectors now ordering more sets than they wanted for their own collections. They simply assumed that buying a few extra sets would pay off nicely in just a couple of years. For a while, at least, they were correct.

The 1955 Proof set was a winner in a couple of respects. For one thing, the half dollar was coined only at the Philadelphia Mint that year, and both the Proof and circulation pieces had attractively low mintages. For variety collectors, some of the sets included nickels having a tripled-die reverse, this being most evident in the word AMERICA. Though this variety was not noticed right away, it became a favorite of savvy collectors who, some years later, would go through set after set looking for it.

Like the cent of 1954, Philadelphia Mint nickels dated 1955 and coined for circulation are often seen a bit dark, as made. Again, this does not seem to have affected the Proof coinage, because greater care was taken in the selection of planchets.

Once again, an increase in mintage over 1954 led to a slightly greater availability of cameo and deep cameo Proofs. These coins also enjoy a higher survival rate in gem condition due to the introduction of soft pliofilm packaging.

Collectors are cautioned against an old fraud that was once commonplace with respect to the "flat-pack" Proof sets of mid-1955 through 1964. A speculative fever developed during the late 1950s in sets that had never had their manila mailing envelopes opened. How this made the coins inside more desirable was never fully explained, but it prompted some dishonest persons to steam open these mailers, replace the coins with washers or slugs, and then reseal the envelopes. Quite a few of these gutted sets traded hands before curious owners could no longer stand the suspense and opened their sets to discover the fraud.

669,384 Complete Sets Possible

Denomination	PF-66		PF-66 Cameo		PF-66 Ultra Cameo	
	Cert. Population	Value	Cert. Population	Value	Cert. Population	Value
Cent (Red)	282		74		19	
Nickel	190		108		3	
Dime	227		58		7	
Quarter	411		122		32	
Half Dollar, Type 1	133		13		0	
Half Dollar, Type 2	1,744		323		77	
Complete Set, Type 1 Half Dollar		$175		$625		$3,000
Complete Set, Type 2 Half Dollar		$70		$250		$250

Original Price: $2.10

Uncertified Value: $75

Original Packaging: The five coins were sealed into a single pliofilm envelope with pockets for each coin, a sixth pocket containing an embossed and printed paper seal reading US MINT PHILADELPHIA in blue on a silver background. The set was protected from damage by two strips of cardstock, and all three pieces were inserted, along with a brief fact sheet, into a buff-colored mailing envelope. This carried a pre-printed return address and a discreet notation of its contents.

Commentary: As the speculative mania for Proof sets grew, alongside a general increase in the number of coin collectors, sales of Proof sets for 1956 nearly doubled in sales from the previous year. There was a great investment interest in these sets, and those who had ordered sets at $2.10 could sell "futures" at $2.50 or more, pending delivery.

The exclusive use of pliofilm packaging for this and subsequent Proof sets through 1964 led to a much higher survival rate in gem condition. Indeed, prices for top-grade certified Proofs are somewhat lower for this and later dates.

Also more abundant, though still not common, are cameo Proofs. The Mint produced some truly amazing, ultra cameo Proofs in 1956. While these represent the best of the best, coins having enough contrast to be certified simply as "cameo" are much more readily available than for earlier dates.

A small number of the Proof nickels dated 1956 were coined with a doubled-die obverse. This is evident as slight doubling in the motto IN GOD WE TRUST.

Another highly desirable variety for this date is the Proof half dollar having the old reverse used from 1950 to 1955. The original reverse hub for the Franklin half dollar featured an eagle that was not sharply rendered. This hub was replaced early in 1956 with one having a very distinctly sculpted eagle, and Proofs dated 1956 of the first variety are very scarce. These varieties may be distinguished fairly easily: the Type 1 reverse has a weak eagle with four narrow feathers visible to the left of its perch, while the Type 2 reverse shows a bold eagle having just three more prominent feathers to the left of the perch. Proofs of all subsequent dates have only this new reverse, though the coins made for circulation may be found with either reverse, since retired Proof dies were used to coin circulation pieces at the Philadelphia Mint.

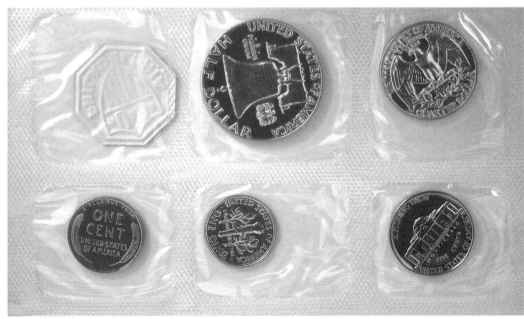

1,247,952 Complete Sets Possible

Denomination	PF-66		PF-66 Cameo		PF-66 Ultra Cameo	
	Cert. Population	Value	Cert. Population	Value	Cert. Population	Value
Cent (Red)	391		78		8	
Nickel	305		20		1	
Dime	301		57		8	
Quarter	410		114		22	
Half Dollar	2,465		339		45	
Complete Set		$115		$325		$1,500

Original Price: $2.10

Uncertified Value: $35

Original Packaging: The five coins were sealed into a single pliofilm envelope with pockets for each coin, a sixth pocket containing an embossed and printed paper seal reading US MINT PHILADELPHIA in blue on a silver background. The set was protected from damage by two strips of cardstock, and all three pieces were inserted, along with a brief fact sheet, into a buff-colored mailing envelope. This carried a pre-printed return address and a discreet notation of its contents.

Commentary: Sales of Proof sets in 1957 nearly doubled, yet again. This time, however, the speculative trading in these popular sets seems to have been its own undoing. Collectors were alarmed at a mintage exceeding a million sets, believing that this was too many for the coins to have any lasting value. In fact, the speculative mania had already subsided before this bomb was dropped. The market simply ran out of new buyers, and when those holding sets wanted to cash in, the market fell.

It has long been suggested, without any evidence to support it, that the Mint, having grown resentful of this speculation, exacted its revenge by overproducing these sets to meet every one of its orders. This is in contrast to previous years, when the Mint refunded orders that it believed exceeded its capacity to produce sets. Whatever the reason behind this very high mintage for the time, it had a chilling effect on the following year's sales. For many years, the 1957 Proof set remained a drug on the market, though it currently enjoys equal favor with contemporary sets, its once shocking mintage no longer seeming so unusual.

Though more Proof coins were made this year than in 1956, the Mint may have used no greater number of dies. Coins struck from severely overpolished and indistinct dies are commonplace for this date, while cameo and deep cameo pieces are somewhat scarcer than for 1956. The smart shopper will examine 1957 Proof coins carefully for such careless production, rather than relying solely on the grade assigned.

On the plus side, a very scarce variety may be found among 1957 Proof nickels. Classified as a quadrupled-die obverse, the extra outlines to LIBERTY and the date will require magnification to discern, but this variety is highly sought by specialists.

An interesting sidebar story concerns the nickels of 1957. For this and the following year, the Mint increased the size of the star that serves as a stop between LIBERTY and the date. This was likely accomplished by hand cutting it to a larger size on the obverse master dies for those dates. In 1959, this star reverted to its 1938 to 1956 size, as found on the obverse master hub for this coin type. Both Proof and currency strikes received this same treatment, and there are no transitional varieties for 1957 and 1958, yet it remains a distinctive and curious footnote to the Jefferson series.

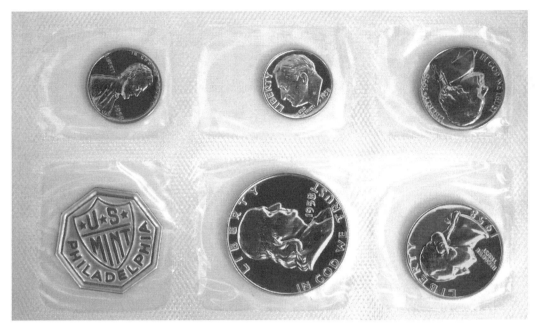

875,652 Complete Sets Possible

Denomination	PF-66		PF-66 Cameo		PF-66 Ultra Cameo	
	Cert. Population	Value	Cert. Population	Value	Cert. Population	Value
Cent (Red)	255		125		19	
Nickel	184		27		1	
Dime	198		65		1	
Quarter	326		97		14	
Half Dollar	1,729		387		9	
Complete Set		$150		$225		$1,700

Original Price: $2.10

Uncertified Value: $75

Original Packaging: The five coins were sealed into a single pliofilm envelope with pockets for each coin, a sixth pocket containing an embossed and printed paper seal reading US MINT PHILADELPHIA in blue on a silver background. The set was protected from damage by two strips of cardstock, and all three pieces were inserted, along with a brief fact sheet, into a buff-colored mailing envelope. This carried a pre-printed return address and a discreet notation of its contents.

Commentary: Taking 1957's spike in sales out of the equation, the number of Proof sets delivered in 1958 is probably just what it would have been in the course of normal growth in the coin collecting hobby. For collectors of the time, however, the drop-off from 1957's mintage seemed to bring an end to the speculation in Proof sets as commodities rather than numismatic items. This setback proved to be only temporary, as the following year's sales would demonstrate. In the meantime, although investors retreated to the sidelines or left the stadium altogether, interest in collecting other specialties continued to be strong.

1958 proved to be the final year of the Lincoln cent's original reverse design, though this was not known to collectors until December, well after the cut-off of Proof set orders. Thus, it had no impact on initial sales, though it did influence the secondary market to some degree in later years.

The nation underwent a brief but distressing economic recession during 1957 and 1958, and this led to some relatively low production figures for the Philadelphia Mint's circulating coinage of 1958. Though this had no direct bearing on the rarity of that year's Proofs, it did lend a certain cachet to all Philadelphia Mint coins dated 1958.

Cameo pieces form a minority of this year's Proof coins, but they are usually available for a premium. As with nearly all issues of 1936 through 1970, ultra or deep cameo Proofs are quite rare. Most of the 1958 Proofs have fully brilliant fields and devices, with destructive overpolishing of the dies being quite common.

Collector's Notebook – 1958
Reverse of Lincoln Wheat Ears cent

The Wheat Ears reverse of the Lincoln cent ended its 50-year run with neither a bang nor a whimper. At 250 million+ coins, its circulation strike mintage was high, but not outrageously so: the previous three years had seen higher. On the Proof side, too, the quantity was only the second-highest of the series, about 2/3 the number struck in 1957. Soon, however, even the greatest annual records of the Wheat Ears cent would be eclipsed by the massive mintages of its Lincoln Memorial successor—in the billions.

Denomination	PF-66		PF-66 Cameo		PF-66 Ultra Cameo	
	Cert. Population	Value	Cert. Population	Value	Cert. Population	Value
Cent (Red)	247		110		31	
Nickel	213		40		4	
Dime	187		60		4	
Quarter	331		11		8	
Half Dollar	1,890		281		11	
Complete Set		$60		$325		$4,000

Original Price: $2.10

Uncertified Value: $30

Original Packaging: The five coins were sealed into a single pliofilm envelope with pockets for each coin, a sixth pocket containing an embossed and printed paper seal reading US MINT PHILADELPHIA in blue on a silver background. The set was protected from damage by two strips of cardstock, and all three pieces were inserted, along with a brief fact sheet, into a buff-colored mailing envelope. This carried a pre-printed return address and a discreet notation of its contents.

Commentary: Sales of Proof sets rebounded in 1959, collectors perhaps being reinvigorated by the relatively lower figure in 1958. It is doubtful that there were more than a quarter million serious coin collectors in the USA at that time, so many of these sets represent multiple orders from single individuals as well as casual orders from the general public.

Anticipation of the new Lincoln Memorial cent was very high, and this certainly contributed to Proof set sales. The new reverse was richly detailed and looked quite sharp on Proofs coined from unworn and properly polished dies. This is in sharp contrast to the obverse of the cent, which by 1959 had lost nearly all of its once superb detail. The same obverse master hub had been cranking out master dies since 1916, when the last major update to the design occurred, and repeated sinking of dies had worn away just about all of Lincoln's beard. He now seemed to have simply a very large and misshapen chin!

Both the nickel and the half dollar had likewise suffered some loss of detail over the years, a fact that was painfully evident when examining Proofs. These coins should have been the very epitome of quality, yet they were often not much sharper than ones made for general circulation.

Cameo coins of this date are especially scarce. Ultra cameo pieces are genuinely rare, as their high prices suggest.

Sharp-eyed collectors should look out for the doubled-die obverse 1959 Proof quarter. It shows distinct doubling of IN GOD WE TRUST.

Collector's Notebook – 1959
Lincoln Memorial cent reverse

150 years after Abraham Lincoln was born in a log cabin on the Kentucky frontier, the national memorial to the president was featured on the reverse of the cent that bore his portrait. Within 10 years, the Lincoln cent would be minted in the multiple billions of coins annually, with Proofs struck in the millions. In 1959, though, the series started with a humble quantity of about 1,150,000 Proofs—humble, but still more than five times the number of all one-cent coins struck for circulation the year Honest Abe was born.

1,691,602 Complete Sets Possible

Denomination	Proof 66		Proof 66 Cameo		Proof 66 Ultra Cameo	
	Cert. Population	Value	Cert. Population	Value	Cert. Population	Value
Cent, Small Date	422		56		11	
Cent, Large Date	248		60		26	
Nickel	272		66		9	
Dime	327		133		42	
Quarter	513		190		63	
Half Dollar	2,073		617		107	
Complete Set, Small Date Cent		$50		$110		$375
Complete Set, Large Date Cent		$40		$100		$325

Original Price: $2.10   **Uncertified Value:** $50 (Small Date cent); $22 (Large Date cent)

Original Packaging: The five coins were sealed into a single pliofilm envelope with pockets for each coin, a sixth pocket containing an embossed and printed paper seal reading US MINT PHILADEL-PHIA in blue on a silver background. The set was protected from damage by two strips of cardstock, and all three pieces were inserted, along with a brief fact sheet, into a buff-colored mailing envelope. This carried a pre-printed return address and a discreet notation of its contents.

Commentary: Proof set sales in 1960 showed healthy, though unspectacular, growth over those of 1959. Midway through the year, however, most collectors were wishing that they had ordered more sets, when the discovery of the Small Date cents set the hobby afire.

Though many veteran numismatists and the Mint itself tried to deny that there was a difference between the Small Date and Large Date cents, sharp-eyed collectors knew better. These varieties are indeed the result of the Mint's using two different obverse master dies in 1960. The Small Date cents came first. Their production was discontinued as early as February of that year, when it was discovered that the small size of the numeral 0 in the date subjected it to chipping and filling of the die. A new master die was quickly introduced in which the numerals 960 were all enlarged to reduce die failure. Both Proofs and circulation pieces were produced of both varieties, but the Small Date coins of both issues were much scarcer. A great speculation arose in 1960 Small Date cents, which spurred what became the great coin investment boom that lasted until 1964.

This date is rich in doubled-die varieties, including cents in which the Small Date and Large Date overlap one another in various combinations, such as Small over Large Date and vice versa. Amazingly, both such combinations are known in Proof! Though not great rarities, these varieties are extremely desirable and carry substantial premiums.

1960 proved to be a troublesome year for die-making at the Mint, as doubled dies are known in Proof for all five denominations. A quadrupled-die reverse is known for the nickel, along with several lesser doubled dies. The Proof dimes may be found with die doubling on either obverse or reverse, both of these being visible to the naked eye. Though not as dramatic, a popular doubled-die reverse is known for Proof 1960 quarters, along with a number of lesser doubling varieties. Finally, a very obvious doubled-die obverse may be found on 1960 Proof half dollars. Given the fact that many Proof sets of this year are still in the hands of persons who don't know of these varieties, the chance for scoring a winning variety at the price of a regular set remains a tantalizing prospect for the knowledgeable shopper.

Best of all is to find these varieties on coins having cameo frosting. This is not impossible, since the overall quality of Proof sets improved markedly beginning in 1960. The Mint was less likely to overuse and overpolish the dies, so it is evident that the dies were being replaced more frequently (perhaps this also accounts for the greater number of varieties). Ultra or deep cameo Proofs are still rare, but they become more readily available beginning with 1960.

As further evidence that the Mint was becoming conscious of the quality of its coins, several minor improvements were made to the dies themselves. The nickel, quarter, and half dollar all received slight facelifts, as the Proofs of these denominations showed obviously greater sharpness than even the best struck 1959 coins. The Roosevelt dime had not suffered any visible erosion of its master hubs since being introduced in 1946, so no changes were needed for it. Sadly, however, the obverse of the cent continued to deteriorate, and its faults were not addressed until 1969.

3,028,244 Complete Sets Possible

Denomination	PF-66		PF-66 Cameo		PF-66 Ultra Cameo	
	Cert. Population	Value	Cert. Population	Value	Cert. Population	Value
Cent	344		62		20	
Nickel	351		59		6	
Dime	284		70		16	
Quarter	504		182		69	
Half Dollar	3,242		631		66	
Complete Set		$40		$70		$300

Original Price: $2.10

Uncertified Value: $12

Original Packaging: The five coins were sealed into a single pliofilm envelope with pockets for each coin, a sixth pocket containing an embossed and printed paper seal reading US MINT PHILADELPHIA in blue on a silver background. The set was protected from damage by two strips of cardstock, and all three pieces were inserted, along with a brief fact sheet, into a buff-colored mailing envelope. This carried a pre-printed return address and a discreet notation of its contents.

Commentary: Collectors and speculators, perhaps still in a state of excitement over the 1960 Small Date cents, ordered a record number of Proof sets this year. The Mint again nearly doubled its output, coming at a time when reports of regional shortages of circulating coins were emerging. This problem was largely overlooked by the hobby in 1961, but it would have serious repercussions on the collecting of Proof coins just a few years later.

1961 is another date notable for doubling varieties. A tripled-die reverse is known for a minority of the 1961 nickels. Though very slight and affecting only the lettering, it is still a popular one with specialists and may be found unattributed within sets priced at regular levels. By far the biggest score for 1961 would be to find one of the rare Proof half dollars having a spectacularly doubled reverse. So obvious is the doubling in E PLURIBUS UNUM that it is hard to believe such coins ever left the Philadelphia Mint undetected. Obviously, this error was caught before many coins were issued, as this variety remains quite rare. All of these varieties are especially rare having cameo contrast.

As for normal Proofs of this date having cameo and deep cameo contrast, the story is much the same as for 1960. Though representing only a tiny percentage of the coins made, enough dies were used this year to produce a small but collectible pool of frosty coins. As always, the overall grade of a coin will factor into its value, as cameo and deep cameo pieces were subject to the same mishandling and poor storage by collectors as their less distinguished siblings. Remember, it was not until comparatively recently that cameo and ultra cameo Proofs have received the respect they deserve.

Collector's Notebook – 1961

Reverse of Washington quarter

By 1961 the Washington quarter had been around for nearly 30 years. Proof mintages had ascended into the millions, with more than 3 million struck per annum in what were the dying years of the silver quarter dollar. In 1961 the denomination was celebrating its 165th birthday, but with the price of silver rising, its days of precious metal were numbered. By 1965, the .900 fine silver workhorse of the American economy was put out to pasture, replaced by a somewhat less pedigreed copper-nickel ringer.

3,218,019 Complete Sets Possible

Denomination	PF-66		PF-66 Cameo		PF-66 Ultra Cameo	
	Cert. Population	Value	Cert. Population	Value	Cert. Population	Value
Cent	313		95		32	
Nickel	361		76		7	
Dime	320		145		30	
Quarter	627		416		101	
Half Dollar	3,912		1,786		351	
Complete Set		$40		$60		$200

Original Price: $2.10

Uncertified Value: $12

Original Packaging: The five coins were sealed into a single pliofilm envelope with pockets for each coin, a sixth pocket containing an embossed and printed paper seal reading US MINT PHILADELPHIA in blue on a silver background. The set was protected from damage by two strips of cardstock, and all three pieces were inserted, along with a brief fact sheet, into a buff-colored mailing envelope. This carried a pre-printed return address and a discreet notation of its contents.

Commentary: Sales of Proof sets in 1962 were similar to that of the previous year. The Mint was not able to fill every order received, as it set itself a certain capacity for Proof coin production and did not exceed it. In the 1960s, Proof coins were still being made under funding provided by the Mint's annual appropriation from Congress, and the profits from their sale did not go toward the Mint's operating expenses. Thus, the Mint had to balance its allocation between circulating coinage and the manufacture of collector coins. As demand for the former increased multifold during the early 1960s, sales of Proof coins were held in check and ultimately discontinued after 1964.

The Proof coins of 1962 did not yield any significant varieties. Perhaps the embarrassing doubled-die reverse half dollar of the previous year prompted more careful die preparation.

Cameo and deep cameo Proofs are somewhat more readily available for this date than for previous ones. The generally superior craftsmanship displayed by the U.S. Mint in its production of Proof coins beginning in 1960 continued through 1964. While certainly not common, both cameo and deep cameo Proofs are collectible for all five denominations. Severely worn or overpolished dies are seldom evident in the 1960 through 1964 Proofs.

One possibility for why the U.S. Mint improved its product may have been the growing popularity of Canadian coins among American collectors. Canada's Ottawa Mint consistently manufactured coins of vastly superior quality to United States Proofs of the 1950s and '60s, and ever more American hobbyists were adding their names to its mailing list at this time.

Collector's Notebook – 1962
Franklin half dollar, obverse

1962 marked the heyday of the Franklin half dollar—that homespun, homely cousin of the beautiful Liberty Walking half that was retired 15 years earlier. In 1962, a record number of Franklin Proofs was struck: more than 3.2 million. While a penny saved might be a penny earned, as advised by the famous author of *Poor Richard's Almanack*, a 1962 Proof half dollar saved would earn its possessor about $25 on today's market, in Proof-65.

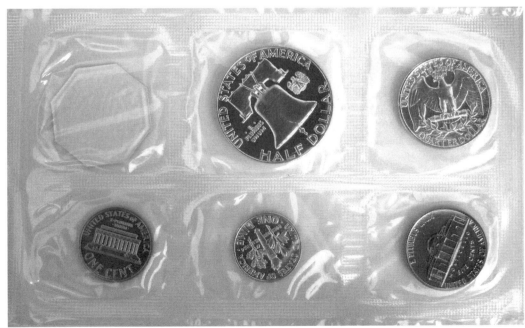

3,075,645 Complete Sets Possible

Denomination	PF-66		PF-66 Cameo		PF-66 Ultra Cameo	
	Cert. Population	Value	Cert. Population	Value	Cert. Population	Value
Cent	293		89		34	
Nickel	319		191		36	
Dime	328		246		86	
Quarter	628		285		109	
Half Dollar	3,661		1,275		245	
Complete Set		$40		$50		$175

Original Price: $2.10

Uncertified Value: $16

Original Packaging: The five coins were sealed into a single pliofilm envelope with pockets for each coin, a sixth pocket containing an embossed and printed paper seal reading US MINT PHILADELPHIA in blue on a silver background. The set was protected from damage by two strips of cardstock, and all three pieces were inserted, along with a brief fact sheet, into a buff-colored mailing envelope. This carried a pre-printed return address and a discreet notation of its contents.

Commentary: Somewhat fewer Proof sets were sold in 1963 than the previous year. This does not reflect any lessened demand. Instead, it just reveals the Mint's estimated capacity for filling orders.

The popularity of coin collecting was at its very height in 1963 and 1964, with sales of coin folders and related hobby products at an all-time high. Proof sets shared in this widespread interest, though the greater focus of speculators at the time was placed on rolls and even bags of Uncirculated, recent-date coinage. As with the Proof set speculation of 1956 and 1957, this fad ultimately collapsed under its own weight, in 1964. Though its demise left many fair-weather collectors holding the bag (literally), the general level of excitement the hobby experienced in the years 1960 to 1964 created more lasting collectors than there had been in the 1950s.

Several doubled-die reverse varieties are known for the Proof dimes of 1963. Three of these are readily discernible with a low-power magnifying glass, and they bring substantial premiums over the value of normal Proofs.

Cameo and deep cameo Proofs are available for all denominations of this date, and both Proof specialists and type collectors eagerly seek them for their beauty. The half dollar is a particular favorite, being the final year of the Franklin/Liberty Bell type. While forming a minority of the more than three million Proofs coined of each denomination, these coins are rare only with deep cameo contrast on both sides. One-sided cameo and deep cameo pieces may be found, too. Though they are worthy of premium prices, grading companies will not certify them with these designations when only one side is frosted. NGC will sometimes award such one-sided cameos its star (*) designation to indicate a coin having superior eye appeal but which does merit labeling as cameo or ultra cameo.

Collector's Notebook – 1963

Franklin half dollar, reverse

The final year of John R. Sinnock's Franklin half dollar design would see a little more than three million Proof coins struck. In the following year the short-lived design would be replaced by a tribute to another great American: President John Kennedy, assassinated in Dallas in November 1963.

3,850,762 Complete Sets Possible

Denomination	PF-66		PF-66 Cameo		PF-66 Ultra Cameo	
	Cert. Population	Value	Cert. Population	Value	Cert. Population	Value
Cent	218		40		33	
Nickel	201		84		8	
Dime	202		77		31	
Quarter	308		81		26	
Half Dollar, Normal Hair	1,931		434		154	
Half Dollar, Accented Hair	440		180		15	
Complete Set, Normal Hair Half Dollar		$40		$50		$175
Complete Set, Accented Hair Half Dollar		$40		$200		$1,000

Original Price: $2.10

Uncertified Value: $12

Original Packaging: The five coins were sealed into a single pliofilm envelope with pockets for each coin, a sixth pocket containing an embossed and printed paper seal reading US MINT PHILADELPHIA in blue on a silver background. The set was protected from damage by two strips of cardstock, and all three pieces were inserted, along with a brief fact sheet, into a buff-colored mailing envelope. This carried a pre-printed return address and a discreet notation of its contents.

Commentary: Responding to the extraordinary demand for the new Kennedy half dollar, the U.S. Mint produced a record for Proof set coinage that would stand for a dozen years. This turned out to be the final year of Proof sets until 1968, as the Mint overreacted to the nationwide coin shortage by suspending Proof coins sales.

While such a large number of Proof coins might be expected to have resulted in poor quality for this date, only a relatively small percentage of 1964 Proof coins reveal worn or overpolished dies. Most of this year's Proofs, of course, have little or no cameo contrast, but that was the norm before the 1970s. Cameo Proofs are available for all denominations, and ultra cameo coins form a small but collectible percentage of the 1964 Proofs. The half dollar is especially sought in such condition, as it is the first year of issue for the Kennedy type. Until a special production for collectors took place beginning in 1992, it was also the only Kennedy half dollar date minted in traditional .900 fine silver.

Given the high mintage for this date, one would expect a greater number of varieties than are actually known. The numeral 9 in the date of the dime features either a pointed or blunt tail, and there are collectors for both. In addition, the dime offers one doubled-die obverse variety, with prominent doubling in the motto IN GOD WE TRUST. A doubled-die obverse for the half dollar likewise is very popular with collectors, though not especially rare.

The most highly sought variety from the 1964 Proof sets is the so-called "Accented Hair" half dollar. It appears that a single working hub had a few extra lines added to Kennedy's hair above his ear, and this feature was transferred to one or more working dies for Proofs alone. While most of the hair on Kennedy's head appears in raised lines, these additional lines are incused. They form a curving shape that is similar to a wishbone that has been split evenly in two and are best seen by holding the coin so that Kennedy's face is pointing toward the light source. This popular variety commands a premium price, especially when found with cameo or deep cameo contrast. The latter is quite rare.

1965 SPECIAL MINT SET

2,360,000 Complete Sets Possible

Denomination	PF-66		PF-66 Cameo		PF-66 Ultra Cameo	
	Cert. Population	Value	Cert. Population	Value	Cert. Population	Value
Cent	278		20		0	
Nickel	365		176		9	
Dime	178		21		0	
Quarter	361		42		0	
Half Dollar	812		276		10	
Special Mint Set		$50		$650		$7,500

Original Price: $4

Uncertified Value: $14

Original Packaging: For 1965 alone, the Special Mint Sets were delivered in packaging that differed little from that used for recent Proof sets. The five coins were sealed in a single pliofilm envelope with pockets for each coin, while a sixth pocket contained a blue plastic token. This featured a silhouette of the Mint eagle and the words UNITED STATES SPECIAL MINT SET, both heat-stamped in metallic silver. The set was protected from damage by two strips of cardstock, and all three pieces were inserted, along with a brief fact sheet, into a white mailing envelope. This carried a pre-printed return address and a discreet notation of its contents.

Because the Special Mint Sets were produced at the San Francisco Assay Office (as the San Francisco Mint was renamed in 1958), its return address appeared on the mailing envelope and shipping boxes, in place of the Philadelphia Mint address used previously.

Commentary: It was announced by the Treasury Department in mid-1964 that no Proof sets would be offered the following year. This action was prompted by a nationwide shortage of circulating coins that caused the Mint great embarrassment and resulted in Congressional finger pointing. Though the problem lay primarily with the too-infrequent collections from payphones and other coin-operated machines, Mint Director Eva Adams was compelled to take action of some kind to placate her critics.

As for the coin collectors who were mistakenly blamed for this shortage, they went through 1965 with neither Proof sets nor their companion Uncirculated sets, commonly called "Mint Sets" by the hobby. Early in 1966, production began in San Francisco on a hybrid coinage that combined features of both. Called "Special Mint Sets" by the Mint, these coins were special only in comparison to regular circulating coinage. Despite being coined at San Francisco, they bore no mintmarks.

As in 1936, and again in 1950, the early deliveries of Special Mint Sets featured coins that were semi-brilliant or satiny. These are highly distinctive, yet they were certainly not equal to Proofs. Later issues dated 1965 featured very brilliant fields, though perhaps not as brilliant as on Proofs. Because the coins were permitted to come into contact with other coins, they suffered numerous tiny marks that further diminished their appeal to collectors. Combined with the fact that only one of the three higher denominations contained any silver, the result was a very disappointing product.

Aggravating the situation further, the Mint set the price of these coins at $4.00 per set. While this may have been more in line with actual cost than the ludicrously small figure of $2.10 still being charged for Proof sets as late as 1964, it only added insult to injury.

As noted above, there are really two finishes to the 1965 Special Mint Sets, the only date of these sets to come both ways. While the specialist will be attracted to this distinction and want to include examples of both, most collectors prefer the brilliant finish that is more akin to actual Proof coinage. These latter coins are also known with cameo and even ultra cameo frosting, though such pieces are far more rare than for the Proof coins of 1960 through 1964.

1966 SPECIAL MINT SET

Coins shown at 90% actual size

Coins shown at 90% actual size

2,261,583 Complete Sets Possible

Denomination	PF-66		PF-66 Cameo		PF-66 Ultra Cameo	
	Cert. Population	Value	Cert. Population	Value	Cert. Population	Value
Cent	250		42		1	
Nickel	210		141		17	
Dime	139		30		0	
Quarter	218		75		1	
Half Dollar	514		274		18	
Special Mint Set		$50		$500		$7,000

Original Price: $4

Uncertified Value: $15

Original Packaging: For the first time, the U.S. Mint packaged its collector coins in a rigid plastic holder. A two-piece casing of transparent plastic was fitted around the coins and sonically sealed. Each coin was held in place by a close-fitting hole having a raised rim. Arranged in a single row, these openings were framed by a flexible insert backing of blue plastic. In raised lettering on the front of the casing appeared UNITED STATES SPECIAL MINT and, in smaller letters, PACKAGED BY U.S. MINT. The casing was inserted into a close-fitting cardboard box, which was blue with the words UNITED STATES SPECIAL MINT SET printed on its front in silver.

Commentary: Perhaps it was the complaints over the higher price of Special Mint Sets that prompted the Mint to give collectors a little more value for their money. The hard plastic case for this year's sets was similar to those marketed by the commercial sector for Proof and Uncirculated sets, and it was a decided improvement over the pliofilm packaging of earlier years.

The U.S. Mint spent the first seven months of 1966 coining pieces dated 1964 and 1965. This was done to maintain date continuity and to produce enough of these coins to prevent any rarities. It was not until August 1 that production of 1966-dated coins began, and all the Special Mint Set pieces were coined at the San Francisco Assay Office.

Though a few of this year's SMS coins have somewhat satiny surfaces, the majority is almost fully prooflike in brilliance. The difference between these coins and true Proofs is that these pieces were struck just once, on unpolished planchets. They display fairly strong strikes, yet the lack of a second impression caused some of the flaws inherent in the planchets to remain visible. A second strike would have smoothed out these flaws. The coins were also permitted to come into contact with others, resulting in minor contact marks and abrasions. This accounts for their rarity in high grades.

Many of the 1966 SMS coins are missing details, the most obvious example being the missing designer initials FG (for Frank Gasparro) on the reverse of some half dollars. This was caused by overpolishing of the dies in an attempt to achieve the full brilliance described above.

Another popular variety is the doubled-die obverse half dollar. Bold doubling is seen on Kennedy's profile and to a lesser degree in the motto IN GOD WE TRUST. A similar doubled-die obverse is known for the circulating edition of the 1966 half dollar, too.

Like the 1965 SMS coins, the 1966 issues exist with cameo and ultra cameo frosting, but these are very scarce. Being the only coin still containing the softer metal silver, the half dollar was less destructive to the dies, and these dies retained their frosted cavities longer. The halves are thus more likely to show contrasting fields and devices, and this remained true through 1970.

1967 SPECIAL MINT SET

Coins shown at 90% actual size

Coins shown at 90% actual size

1,863,344 Complete Sets Possible

Denomination	PF-66		PF-66 Cameo		PF-66 Ultra Cameo	
	Cert. Population	Value	Cert. Population	Value	Cert. Population	Value
Cent	208		35		0	
Nickel	205		183		37	
Dime	109		46		2	
Quarter	230		137		8	
Half Dollar	520		545		70	
Special Mint Set		$60		$400		$3,500

Original Price: $4

Uncertified Value: $22

Original Packaging: The same packaging used in 1966 was employed for the 1967 sets. This consisted of a two-piece casing of transparent plastic fitted around the coins and sonically sealed. A blue plastic insert formed a backdrop for the coins, and the sonically sealed holder was slipped into a blue cardboard box imprinted in silver: UNITED STATES SPECIAL MINT SET. The 1967 boxes differ only in the application of a round, white sticker bearing the Treasury Department logo and the date 1967, both printed in blue ink.

Commentary: Though the use of mintmarks remained under suspension during 1967, normal dating of the coins resumed. All of the 1967-dated coinage, including the Special Mint Set pieces, was produced during calendar year 1967.

The San Francisco Assay Office was becoming quite adept at producing this distinctive coinage, and nearly all of the 1967 issues are of a quality that approaches true Proof coinage. Satin-finish coins are unknown for this date, and the typical 1967 SMS coin has a fully brilliant finish. Remarkably, this was achieved without overpolishing the dies and causing them to lose precious details, a problem with many of the 1966 issues. It was a lesson that should have been applied in 1968 when actual Proof coinage resumed.

A popular doubled-die variety is known for the obverse of the quarter. The doubling affects both LIBERTY and IN GOD WE TRUST. Unfortunately, every example this author has seen also has even more obvious strike doubling, the last which adds nothing to the value of a coin. To distinguish between strike doubling and die doubling on this variety, look for a small notch at the lower right corner of the upright of the R in LIBERTY. This notch is found only on true doubled-die coins.

Sales of the 1967 Special Mint Sets were disappointing, but it was not due entirely to the coins. Coin collecting had experienced a drop in popularity since its 1964 peak, and there simply were fewer participants. There was also little expectation of profit in the Special Mint Sets, so purchasers tended to limit their orders to sets they needed for themselves. The earlier practice of putting away extra sets for later resale did not seem to be in effect during the SMS years. The 1967 set has always been the scarcest of the three, though the greater quality seen in these coins as compared to the 1965 to 1966 issues makes them of approximately equal scarcity in gem condition.

Cameo pieces are very difficult to locate for the 1967 issues, while deep or ultra cameo coins are quite rare. This is due primarily to the lower mintage for 1967, fewer dies resulting in fewer cameos.

1968-S

3,041,506 Complete Sets Possible

Denomination	PF-67		PF-67 Cameo		PF-67 Ultra Cameo	
	Cert. Population	Value	Cert. Population	Value	Cert. Population	Value
Cent	178		93		138	
Nickel	163		48		129	
Dime	129		38		33	
Dime, No S	5		0		0	
Quarter	179		86		39	
Half Dollar	300		308		605	
Complete Set		$20		$40		$150

Original Price: $5

Uncertified Value: $7.50 (regular dime); $10,000 (No S dime)

Original Packaging: Rigid plastic was again used, as for the Special Mint Sets of 1966 and 1967, and this has remained the U.S. Mint's standard for Proof sets ever since.

A transparent casing with frosted border and an upper and lower shell housed a black plastic insert with fitted holes for each coin. This insert was not printed or embossed, but the outer casing was. The Mint eagle is embossed on the front shell, while the back carries the words "United States Proof Set" in raised script, with the notation PACKAGED BY U.S. MINT in small, block letters. The assembled set was inserted into a blue cardboard box with a tuck-in flap at its top for ease of opening and closing. The inscription "United States Proof Set • 1968" appears on the box in white script.

So successful was this packaging concept that it has survived to the present day with only superficial changes. Therefore, later packaging will be described only when it is exceptional.

Commentary: Collectors were delighted to learn that mintmarks would return to the nation's coinage beginning in 1968. These letters would henceforth appear on the obverse for all denominations, though this was nothing new for the cent. In a double surprise, the Treasury Department announced that not only would sales of Proof sets resume, but also that these sets were to be made at San Francisco and carry that facility's familiar S mintmark.

The 1968 sets were quickly oversubscribed, the Mint having to return many checks once its production limit had been reached. While a number of collectors were thus disappointed, those who received the 1968-S sets saw them quickly rise in value. Ultimately, these high prices receded, and the 1968-S Proof set spent many years trading at or below its issue price until enjoying a revival of interest during the 1990s.

Much of the initial desirability of this year's set centered around the Proof-only San Francisco Mint dimes, quarters, and halves. Completing a series of these coin types now required that the S-Mint Proofs be included, and the manufacturers of coin albums were prompted to issue two versions for each of these series—one having the Proof-only coins and one without them.

A major rarity resulted when an obverse die for the Proof dime was shipped to San Francisco without a mintmark. Amazingly, despite the care with which Proof dies were to be inspected, no one seems to have noticed this omission until after it produced an unknown number of coins. Someone inspecting finished coins eventually spotted this error, but it was too late to prevent shipment of an unknown number of sets including this error coin.

In its eagerness to distinguish these true Proofs from the SMS coins of 1965 to 67, the San Francisco Assay Office overpolished most of the dies. The result was that these coins, while pleasingly brilliant, often reveal mushy details.

Varieties for this year's set include a slight doubled-die obverse for the cent, visible on the date and LIBERTY. Also highly collectible is the Proof nickel having a clearly repunched mintmark. Prominent doubled-dies are known for both the obverse and reverse of the dime, and they may be detected by examining the lettering of each. The quarter has a slight doubled-die obverse variety, with the date and lettering affected, though it is difficult to distinguish. Better is the doubled-die reverse variety, which is plainly evident in the value QUARTER DOLLAR. Finally, the motto IN GOD WE TRUST is doubled on some of the 1968-S half dollars.

Cameo and ultra cameo Proofs, while they form a minority of the 1968 issues, are not especially rare. They remain, however, highly desirable.

In an interesting footnote to the 1968 Proof Program, the dies for these coins were subsequently sold to a scrap metal dealer in nearby South San Francisco, the author's hometown. Though partially defaced with a blowtorch, the dies remained sufficiently interesting that a quick thinking entrepreneur purchased them and offered the dies to collectors at a considerable mark-up. While once commonplace in the coin market, these dies are now well dispersed and command good prices. Their value is dependent on the amount of the design visible, fully defaced dies being worth much less. Among the several hundred believed to exist, they range in value from $50 for a cent die to as much as $500 for a half dollar. Though U.S. Mint dies of most years are illegal to own, the Secret Service has never challenged the legality of the 1968 Proof dies, since their official disposal is well documented.

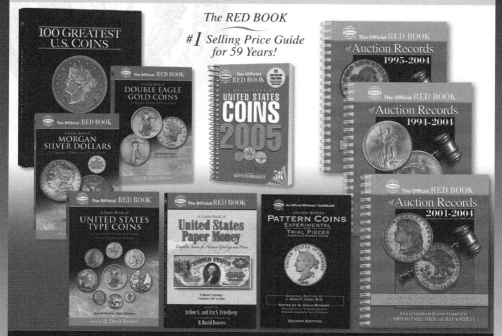

2,934,631 Complete Sets Possible

Denomination	PF-67		PF-67 Cameo		PF-67 Ultra Cameo	
	Cert. Population	Value	Cert. Population	Value	Cert. Population	Value
Cent	141		70		154	
Nickel	145		63		145	
Dime	105		44		33	
Quarter	144		113		50	
Half Dollar	330		451		673	
Complete Set		$20		$40		$140

Original Price: $5

Uncertified Value: $8

Original Packaging: A transparent plastic casing surrounded a black plastic insert containing the coins. This was inserted into a blue cardboard box upon which, in white script, appears "United States Proof Set • 1969". The tuck-in flap at the top of the box was used for some of this year's sets, but a new design having a flap on the face of the box was transitioned for the 1969 sets.

Commentary: Like the 1968-S sets before them, the 1969-S Proof sets were ordered in much greater numbers than the Mint could produce. Disappointed collectors and speculators had to watch in frustration as these sets were bid up to $15 in the months following their arrival. Just like the previous year's sets, however, these too fell in value once the initial fever subsided. This history has dogged them ever since, and the current low price for Mint-sealed sets seems a bargain. These sets certainly did not prove to be a good long-term investment for those who purchased them at issue price, unless they were fortunate to receive sets that included cameo coins.

The 1969-S Proof coins are of similar appearance to those dated 1968-S, but they are much less likely to reveal a loss of detail due to overpolished dies. The cent in particular looks quite sharp, as the Mint created an entirely new obverse hub for 1969. This came after years of deterioration in Lincoln's portrait, made all too evident by the 1968 Proofs.

The only interesting varieties for this date are found on the quarter. These include a triple-punched mintmark, as well as a doubled-die obverse affecting the date and LIBERTY.

Following a trend that began with the resumption of Proof coinage the previous year, cameo and ultra cameo coins are more readily available than they are for Proofs of earlier times. The Mint seems to have changed dies more frequently to prevent their erosion, and fresh dies resulted in coins having frosted legends and devices. Collectors at this time were just beginning to appreciate cameo coins, though the premiums attached to such pieces today were unknown then. It was a time when the discriminating collector could pick up a future bargain whose value was not even suspected by the seller.

2,632,810 Complete Sets Possible

Denomination	PF-67		PF-67 Cameo		PF-67 Ultra Cameo	
	Cert. Population	Value	Cert. Population	Value	Cert. Population	Value
Cent, Small Date	128		57		36	
Cent, Large Date	170		63		64	
Nickel	155		102		103	
Dime	119		88		54	
Dime, No S	45		12		0	
Quarter	190		93		22	
Half Dollar	289		442		351	
Complete Set, Large Date Cent		$22		$40		$140
Complete Set, Small Date Cent		$150		$275		$750

Original Price: $5

Uncertified Value: $110 (Small Date cent); $18 (Large Date cent); $1,600 (No S dime)

Original Packaging: A transparent plastic casing surrounded a black plastic insert containing the coins. This was inserted into a blue cardboard box upon which, in white script, appears "United States Proof Set • 1970."

Commentary: As in 1960, two different obverse hubs were employed to sink dies for the cent's obverse. Quickly labeled "Small Date" and "Large Date" by the hobby, the distinctions were not so obvious. Some collectors have come to recognize the Small Date variety as the "Level 7" variety, since the tops of the 7 and the 0 are even with one another. On the more common Large Date variety, the 0 is distinctly taller than the 7.

The unthinkable happened again in 1970, when the Philadelphia Mint shipped an S-less die for the obverse of the dime to San Francisco. Polished up and placed into a coin press, it went to work striking Proofs that bore no mintmark. As before, the error was spotted only after some coins had been shipped to customers, the Mint providing an estimate of 2,200 such sets having been delivered. Given the small number of pieces certified to date, the actual net mintage of this variety is probably lower than the figure quoted.

Less dramatic varieties include several doubled obverse dies, the most interesting of these having the Large Date impressed over the Small Date. This same situation occurred in 1960, and both years are popular with specialists.

The quality of 1970-S Proof sets is generally very high, though the level of perfection achieved in the 1980s and later was simply unknown at this time. Cameo and deep cameo coins are not common for this date, but they are readily collectible for those willing to pay the appropriate premium. Undoubtedly, there are still unsearched Proof sets in the hands of persons who purchased them from the Mint in 1970, so the prospect of cherrypicking cameo coins among these sets remains.

The year 1970 marked the last time that silver was used in a United States coin intended for circulation. As it turned out, however, circulating half dollars of this date were never produced because legislation to change their composition to copper-nickel clad was pending most of the year. Not passed until the final week of 1970, this bill held up production of half dollars and ultimately limited their coinage to the number needed to fulfill orders from collectors for Uncirculated and Proof sets. The appeal of the last silver half dollar is such that this year's Proof set has commanded a premium over the comparable 1968 and 1969 sets ever since.

While error-strike coins are not generally featured in this book, it is worth noting one particular exception. A single 1970-S quarter is known struck over a worn silver quarter dated 1900! At this time, the U.S. Mint was withdrawing and melting obsolete silver coins, and it has been suggested that one of these pieces remained in a hopper that was later loaded with planchets intended for Proof quarters. However, investigation revealed that it was a novelty made by an employee of the San Francisco Mint and quietly sold to a California coin dealer, who soon resold it. The coin was confiscated by the Secret Service.

3,220,733 Complete Sets Possible

Denomination	PF-67		PF-67 Cameo		PF-67 Ultra Cameo	
	Cert. Population	Value	Cert. Population	Value	Cert. Population	Value
Cent	183		70		54	
Nickel	122		91		71	
Nickel, No S	12		24		7	
Dime	79		47		4	
Quarter	134		62		3	
Half Dollar	290		148		28	
Complete Set, Normal Nickel		$20		$35		$300
Complete Set, No S Nickel		$1,100		$1,300		$1,600

Original Price: $5

Uncertified Value: $6; $1,400 (No S nickel)

Original Packaging: A transparent plastic casing surrounded a black plastic insert containing the coins. This was inserted into a blue cardboard box upon which, in white script, appears "United States Proof Set • 1971."

Commentary: At the time orders were being taken for 1971 Proof sets, in the fall of 1970, the aftermarket prices for the 1968 to 1970 sets were still quite high. Collectors and speculators, seeking another windfall, ordered a large number of sets for 1971. Perhaps due to disappointment with the new copper-nickel clad half dollar, and despite the fact that San Francisco Mint nickels were now available only as Proofs, the value of this year's set never really advanced. More than 30 years later, after adjusting for inflation, uncertified 1971-S Proof sets seem quite a bargain.

The nickel was significantly modified for 1971, receiving new master hubs for both obverse and reverse. While its overall relief was lowered, its details were rendered more distinctly. This also extended the life of the dies. Though done primarily for the benefit of the circulating coinage, it gave a very different look to the Proof nickels of this and subsequent years.

By accident at the Philadelphia Mint, where all dies for all mints were made, the S mintmark was omitted from one die for nickel Proofs, and an estimated 1,655 coins were delivered in sets before any remaining error coins were retrieved and melted. Also popular, though worth not nearly as much, are several doubled-die obverse varieties for the cent, which exhibit doubling in the date and lettering. Finally, a very distinctive doubled-die obverse may be found on the half dollar, affecting the motto IN GOD WE TRUST.

The half dollars of this date were the first to be coined in the copper-nickel clad composition that had been standard for dimes and quarters since 1965. The harder alloy required some modifications to the half dollar, the most obvious being a reduction in the overall size of Kennedy's portrait. The new coins also displayed much broader borders.

It was about this time that the Mint began chromium-plating its dies for Proof coins. Not only did this enhance their wearing quality, permitting a greater number of strikes per die, but it also increased the number of coins that would possess some degree of frosting on their raised elements before this feature wore away. Though it is not really evident in examining 1971 Proofs, as the high certified value of cameo and ultra cameo coins confirms, it resulted in much nicer Proofs the following year.

3,260,996 Complete Sets Possible

Denomination	PF-67		PF-67 Cameo		PF-67 Ultra Cameo	
	Cert. Population	Value	Cert. Population	Value	Cert. Population	Value
Cent	81		77		38	
Nickel	56		84		61	
Dime	48		68		11	
Quarter	69		76		14	
Half Dollar	152		134		58	
Complete Set		$10		$25		$70

Original Price: $5

Uncertified Value: $6

Original Packaging: A transparent plastic casing surrounded a black plastic insert containing the coins. This was inserted into a blue cardboard box upon which, in white script, appears "United States Proof Set • 1972."

Commentary: The Proof set of 1972 is another whose value uncertified has never advanced much. This is entirely a matter of traditional perception, as this set is no more common than later ones of comparable mintage. It is usually cast with the 1968, 1969, and 1971 sets, and, like those dates, it seems something of a bargain.

The Eisenhower dollar, which had been minted for general circulation since late 1971, would not be included in Proof sets until 1973. The sets of 1972 would feature the cent through the half dollar.

A rare variety of the Proof 1972-S cent features doubling on LIBERTY and IN GOD WE TRUST. A note of caution: be careful to distinguish between die doubling, which is highly collectible, and common strike doubling, which adds nothing to the value of a coin. One way to spot strike doubling is to check the mintmark. Since this feature was applied to each die after it was hubbed, it would not share in the die doubling effect. Any doubling seen on a mintmark is usually indicative of strike doubling. The leading (but not all) certification services are aware of doubled-dies vis-à-vis strike doubling, and coins they certify as doubled-dies were made as such.

In the year 1972, cameo coins began to comprise a significant percentage of the Proof mintage. While still outnumbered by fully brilliant pieces, cameo and deep cameo Proofs are sufficiently available to be within the budget of most collectors. Aside from the degree of frosting they possess, the Proofs made before 1978 are of a lesser quality overall, so examples grading above Proof-67 are still scarce.

Collector's Notebook – 1972
Eisenhower dollar, obverse

World War II general (and later president) Dwight David Eisenhower occupies the 1972 dollar in a bold profile portrait. Proof versions of the large, heavy coins were struck only in their 40% silver format this year; in 1973, the copper-nickel clad version would also receive the Proof treatment.

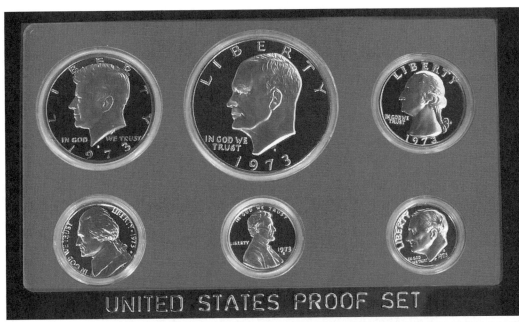

2,760,339 Complete Sets Possible

Denomination	PF-67		PF-67 Cameo		PF-67 Ultra Cameo	
	Cert. Population	Value	Cert. Population	Value	Cert. Population	Value
Cent	33		26		32	
Nickel	28		46		21	
Dime	25		17		1	
Quarter	42		19		9	
Half Dollar	49		62		32	
Dollar	110		122		65	
Complete Set		$22		$35		$70

Original Price: $7

Uncertified Value: $14

Original Packaging: A more elaborate variation of the standard plastic case was adopted for 1973 to coincide with the inclusion of a Proof dollar coin. The clear plastic case was retained, but it included receptacles with raised rims to secure the coins. Serving as a backdrop was a flexible insert covered in red flocking. The transparent holder was encased within a black plastic frame featuring a rigid cover that was attached to it via a hinge at the bottom of the frame. This cover could be swung on its hinges to provide an easel-type display of the set. The words UNITED STATES PROOF SET appeared at the bottom of the frame in raised, silver lettering. The assembled set was inserted into a box of construction similar to that used from 1968 to 1972, but the inscription "United States Proof Set • 1973" was in silver ink on black cardboard.

Commentary: The lackluster price performance of the 1971 and 1972 sets seems to have had an impact on sales this year. Despite the widely heralded inclusion of the Eisenhower dollar in this year's sets, the net mintage of Proofs was down. The price increase from $5 to $7 certainly didn't help matters.

The Eisenhower dollar had been minted for general circulation since 1971, but it debuted in the fall of that year, too late to be included in 1971 Proof sets. Collectors had every reason to expect that this coin would be a part of the 1972 sets, but it was not. There was no technical reason for not including it. Instead, the problem was likely due to the Mint's quaint budgeting procedures. The Mint still operated under an annual appropriation, and money for any additional operations required a supplemental appropriation from Congress. This evidently did not arrive until the 1973 sets were being planned, and it provided for the revised packaging to accommodate the dollar coin.

Though no dollar coins were made for circulation in 1973, this seems to have had little impact on the value of Proofs. By this time, collectors had grown accustomed to the S-Mint, Proof-only coins.

UNITED STATES PROOF SET

2,612,568 Complete Sets Possible

Denomination	Proof 67		Proof 67 Cameo		Proof 67 Ultra Cameo	
	Cert. Population	Value	Cert. Population	Value	Cert. Population	Value
Cent	6		34		49	
Nickel	9		21		49	
Dime	17		13		5	
Quarter	28		21		11	
Half Dollar	32		68		52	
Dollar	80		95		90	
Complete Set		$20		$30		$70

Original Price: $7

Uncertified Value: $10

Original Packaging: The packaging used in 1973 was employed again for the 1974 sets. This consisted of a clear plastic casing with a red, flocked insert and a black, hinged frame. The hinge provided for an easel display of the set, and the words UNITED STATES PROOF SET appeared at the bottom of the frame in raised, silver lettering. A black cardboard box housed the assembled set, and the words "United States Proof Set • 1974" were printed on it in silver script.

Commentary: The Proof sets of 1974 were a replay of 1973 in all respects. They are priced similarly, and they are alike in the appearance of both the coins and the packaging.

The Proof cents of 1974 carry a modified portrait of Lincoln. This was used for all the Proofs and about half of the circulation pieces before yet another obverse appeared later in 1974. It came too late for the Proofs, which had already been delivered, but both portraits may be collected for the circulating cents of this date. The changes are very subtle, and they are best understood by making a side-by-side comparison of the 1973, 1974, and 1975 Proof cents.

The obverse of the quarter was also modified. A fine, high-relief bust of Washington replaced the one used for earlier clad issues, and this same bust continued through the Bicentennial coinage of 1975 and 1976. As with the cent, the differences may seem trivial to the casual viewer, but they are nonetheless worth noting.

Since 1972, cameo coins had made up a growing percentage of each year's output, though most pieces were still of the fully brilliant finish or simply lacked enough cameo contrast on both sides to receive a "cameo" designation from the commercial grading services. Ultra cameo specimens are scarce for this date, a condition that would remain true for United States Proof coins until 1978.

A fact perhaps not evident from the table above is that cameo and ultra cameo coins in grades above PF-67 become increasingly common for dates in the mid-1970s and later. This reflects an increase in the quality of the coins as made, as well as a greater likelihood of their being preserved carefully. The traditional 1950s and '60s practice of breaking open Proof sets to place the coins in albums took its toll on their pristine surfaces. As more collectors came to value Mint-sealed sets or coins certified by third-party grading services, the survival rate of top-notch pieces has been higher.

2,845,450 Complete Sets Possible

Denomination	PF-67		PF-67 Cameo		PF-67 Ultra Cameo	
	Cert. Population	Value	Cert. Population	Value	Cert. Population	Value
Cent	33		26		44	
Nickel	24		33		39	
Dime	21		25		5	
Quarter	59		105		160	
Half Dollar	95		208		210	
Dollar, Type 1	128		143		81	
Complete Set		$25		$35		$70

Original Price: $7

Uncertified Value: $15

Original Packaging: The coins were secured in a clear plastic casing with a red, flocked insert and a black, hinged frame. The hinge provided for an easel display of the set, and the words UNITED STATES PROOF SET appeared at the bottom of the frame in raised, silver lettering. A black cardboard box housed the assembled set, and the words "United States Proof Set • 1975" were printed on it in silver script.

Commentary: No quarters, halves, or dollars dated 1975 were coined. The coins of those denominations minted during 1975 bore a date of 1974 or the dual dates 1776-1976. These latter coins carried distinctive reverse designs in commemoration of the nation's bicentennial. The regular Proof sets sold in 1975 thus consisted of cents and nickels dated 1975-S, as well as the three Bicentennial issues in their regular copper-nickel clad composition.

The Bicentennial coins had only a minimal impact on sales of this year's sets, but the 1975 Proof set still proved to be a winner. It turned out that the popular S mintmark would no longer appear on cents coined there for circulation, though production of anonymous cents continued at San Francisco for another few years. Instead, the only 1975-S cents would be those in the Proof sets, and the value of these sets rose above their issue price almost immediately.

Rumors have persisted for years that a 1975 Proof dime without a mintmark exists, and there may indeed be one or two such coins. This author has not seen one, nor have any been certified. If genuine, this coin is certainly a key rarity in the modern Proof series.

The 1975-S Proof sets all seem to include Type 1 dollars. This subtype features more shallow relief and block lettering on its reverse. This distinctive lettering was included in Dennis R. Williams' winning design for the reverse of the Bicentennial dollar, and the Mint's engraving staff neglected to change it. Critics of the coins noted that this lettering was in conflict with the serif-style lettering of Frank Gasparro's obverse, and it was altered subsequent to delivery of the 1975 sets. The Type 1 dollar is a bit scarcer and carries a slight premium value. The use of *Type* is a misnomer, and *variety* or *subtype* would be more appropriate. However, by tradition, *Type* it is!

1976-S

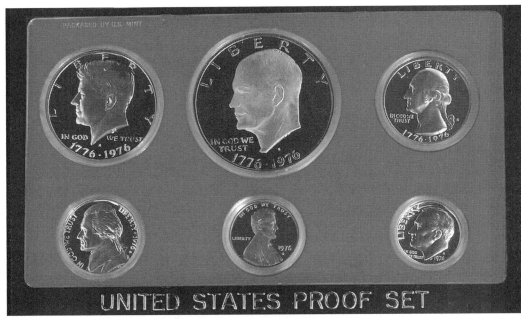

Denomination	PF-67		PF-67 Cameo		PF-67 Ultra Cameo	
	Cert. Population	Value	Cert. Population	Value	Cert. Population	Value
Cent	21		64		145	
Nickel	28		15		90	
Dime	10		49		112	
Quarter	*		*		*	
Half Dollar	*		*		*	
Dollar, Type 2	121		139		219	
Complete Set		$20		$30		$70

*Included in 1975-S population

Original Price: $7

Uncertified Value: $9

Original Packaging: The coins were secured in a clear plastic casing with a red, flocked insert and a black, hinged frame. The hinge provided for an easel display of the set, and the words UNITED STATES PROOF SET appeared at the bottom of the frame in raised, silver lettering. A black cardboard box housed the assembled set, and the words "United States Proof Set • 1976" were printed on it in silver script.

Commentary: The 1976-S Proof set was enormously popular, as it included the three Bicentennial issues and, unlike the 1975 sets, all six coins were dated 1976. This certainly accounts for the unusually large sales. Despite its high mintage, this set retains its popularity with collectors.

It appears that all of the 1976 Proof sets included Type 2 dollars, with slender, serif-style lettering and sharper details on the reverse. While there is no great discrepancy in rarity or value between the two reverse types, the Type 1 dollars are more prized by collectors.

Cameo Proofs dated 1976 may be found with little effort, though *deep* cameo coins are still relatively scarce. Uniformly brilliant Proofs make up a portion of this date's mintage, but their percentage continued to decline as the 1970s progressed.

Collector's Notebook – 1976

Eisenhower Bicentennial dollar, reverse

The official celebration of the nation's bicentennial included new designs for the three largest circulating coins. Almost 18 million Eisenhower dollars were struck in Proof format, both copper-nickel and silver, all at the San Francisco Mint. For years afterward casino gamblers would find the base metal dollars paid out at the slots in Las Vegas, but not the silver versions: the latter were struck only in Proof, for collectors.

1976-S SILVER BICENTENNIAL SET

Denomination	PF-67		PF-67 Cameo		PF-67 Ultra Cameo	
	Cert. Population	Value	Cert. Population	Value	Cert. Population	Value
Quarter	84		177		210	
Half Dollar	142		202		274	
Dollar	224		193		299	
Silver Bicentennial Set		$40		$50		$60

Original Price: $15 (lowered to $12)

Uncertified Value: $19

Original Packaging: Each coin was encased in an acrylic capsule, and these were inserted into a wallet-like display case. This consisted of a blue panel holding the individual capsules, the panel being hinged at its top to permit viewing of both sides of the coins. The panel was attached to the inside of a wallet that folded over to protect the coins. The inside cover of the wallet, opposite the blue panel, was a vibrant red and featured a diagonal ribbon of red, white, and blue stripes. Printed in silver script on this inside cover were the words "United States Bicentennial Silver Proof Set." The outside cover was blue, and it bore the dates 1776-1976 encircled by thirteen stars, all printed in gold ink.

Commentary: The silver clad composition, used for the half dollars of 1965 to 1970 and the collector-edition dollars since 1971, was extended to the three Bicentennial issues. These three-coin sets were sold separately from the regular Proof sets of 1975 and 1976, which included copper-nickel clad Proofs of the quarter, half dollar, and dollar. Initially priced at $15 per set, this price was soon lowered to $12, and rebates were issued to those who had paid the higher figure.

The attractive packaging of this set went a long way toward enhancing sales, and the ordering period lasted many years. The runaway speculation in silver prices that occurred during 1979 and 1980 caused the Mint to suspend sales during this period, but they later resumed and lasted through 1982.

Because silver is a naturally more brilliant metal than the copper-nickel alloy used for the regular Proofs, the mirror finish on these coins is quite a bit more pleasing. This enhances the contrast with the coins' typically frosted devices, so cameo and ultra cameo pieces are readily available. Being a softer alloy, too, the silver clad Proofs were less destructive to dies, which retained their frosting longer.

A rare and possibly unique trial striking of the 1976 silver Proof dollar is known without the S mintmark. Presumably, this was coined at the Philadelphia Mint before the dies were shipped west. No documentation exists to account for this coin, though the coin does certainly exist. This author examined it in 1995, and there was no evidence of alteration.

Collector's Notebook – 1976

Bicentennial quarter dollar, reverse

Millions of Proof Bicentennial quarter dollars were struck in both copper-nickel and silver. However, in spite of the new coin designs, the hobby was in the doldrums in 1976, and these large quantities weren't absorbed into the marketplace. Today, Proofs are common and easy to acquire in gem quality.

UNITED STATES PROOF SET

3,251,152 Complete Sets Possible

Denomination	PF-67		Proof-67 Cameo		Proof-67 Ultra Cameo	
	Cert. Population	Value	Cert. Population	Value	Cert. Population	Value
Cent	22		8		60	
Nickel	19		4		49	
Dime	6		11		9	
Quarter	6		17		33	
Half Dollar	50		42		45	
Dollar	123		66		149	
Complete Set		$30		$40		$50

Original Price: $9

Uncertified Value: $9

Original Packaging: The coins were secured in a clear plastic casing with a red, flocked insert and a black, hinged frame. The hinge provided for an easel display of the set, and the words UNITED STATES PROOF SET appeared at the bottom of the frame in raised, silver lettering. A black cardboard box housed the assembled set, and the words "United States Proof Set • 1977" were printed on it in silver script.

Commentary: Sales of Proof sets receded a bit after the excitement of the Bicentennial period, though this year still enjoyed a fairly large production.

The quality of the 1977 Proof sets was noticeably superior to that of just a few years earlier, with fully struck, richly detailed cameo Proofs being the norm rather than the exception. There are no great rarities for this set, though top-grade, ultra cameo coins still bring strong prices.

The quarter dollar received a facelift for 1977, both its obverse and reverse being revised. The coin's relief was lowered and its details sharpened, the portrait of Washington in particular being clearly different from the high-relief bust used from 1974 to 1976.

Collector's Notebook – 1977
Eisenhower dollar, reverse

The reverse of the Eisenhower dollar might seem a strange anomaly—an American eagle clutching an olive branch on the surface of the moon—unless you know its inspiration: the official insignia of Apollo 11, which made its historic lunar landing a few years earlier. Millions of Proofs were struck in the 1970s.

3,127,781 Complete Sets Possible

Denomination	PF-68 Ultra Cameo		PF-69 Ultra Cameo	
	Cert. Population	Value	Cert. Population	Value
Cent	84		596	
Nickel	159		2,564	
Dime	77		2,873	
Quarter	134		3,037	
Half Dollar	290		4,052	
Dollar	692		3,150	
Complete Set		$60		$110

Original Price: $9

Uncertified Value: $10

Original Packaging: The coins were secured in a clear plastic casing with a red, flocked insert and a black, hinged frame. The hinge provided for an easel display of the set, and the words UNITED STATES PROOF SET appeared at the bottom of the frame in raised, silver lettering. A black cardboard box housed the assembled set, and the words "United States Proof Set • 1978" were printed on it in silver script.

Commentary: Sales in 1978 were down a bit from the previous year, but not enough to have any real impact on rarity.

The quality of United States Proof coins, which had been progressing steadily since 1972, took a giant leap in 1978. It seems that the Mint was now determined to produce cameo Proofs exclusively. Chromium-plating of the dies, combined with quick replacement of those dies that had begun to show wear, maintained a consistent quality throughout this year's production run of Proof sets.

More skillful preparation of the dies also left fewer polishing lines and other flaws. As a result, the certified grades applied to typical Proofs of this and subsequent years are generally higher than for pre-1978 issues.

With this greater uniformity in die preparation came a concurrent reduction in the number of die varieties. In fact, doubled-die obverse and reverse varieties are nearly unknown for Proofs after the early 1970s. Of the few that do exist, most are insignificant in that the doubling is very minor.

Collector's Notebook – 1978
Roosevelt dime, reverse

The Roosevelt dime has been a mainstay of Proof sets since 1950. Proofs of the early 1950s numbered below 100,000 per year, but those quantities quickly grew. By 1956 more than 500,000 Proofs were minted; the million-coin mark was broken in 1959; and by the end of the silver series the annual Proof mintage neared four million. Recent years have seen numbers in the two to three million range, with silver Proofs hovering around a million annually.

3,677,175 Complete Sets Possible

Denomination	PF-68 Ultra Cameo		PF-69 Ultra Cameo	
	Cert. Population	Value	Cert. Population	Value
Cent	181		590	
Nickel	335		1,470	
Dime	118		1,865	
Quarter	255		2,091	
Half Dollar	419		3,140	
Dollar	676		5,162	
Type 1 or Filled S Sets		$60		$110

Included above

Denomination	PF-68 Ultra Cameo		PF-69 Ultra Cameo	
	Cert. Population	Value	Cert. Population	Value
Cent	220		302	
Nickel	169		790	
Dime	88		1,151	
Quarter	174		1,120	
Half Dollar	299		1,401	
Dollar	588		1,603	
Type 2 or Clear S Sets		$200		$300

Original Price: $9

Uncertified Value: $9 (Filled S); $125 (Clear S)

Original Packaging: The coins were secured in a clear plastic casing with a red, flocked insert and a black, hinged frame. The hinge provided for an easel display of the set, and the words UNITED STATES PROOF SET appeared at the bottom of the frame in raised, silver lettering. A black cardboard box housed the assembled set, and the words "United States Proof Set • 1979" were printed on it in silver script.

The Mint did not prepare a new holder for this first year of Susan B. Anthony dollar production. Instead, it simply adapted the existing Proof set holder to accommodate the smaller coin by inserting a clear plastic retaining ring into the large dollar hole.

Commentary: Unlike its delay with the Eisenhower dollar in 1971 and 1972, the Mint did not wait for new holders before including the Susan B. Anthony dollar in this year's Proof sets. The novelty of the mini-dollar clearly boosted sales of Proof sets at a time when interest in them was otherwise lagging.

Until the mid-1980s, the S mintmarks applied to Proof dies were still punched into each die with hand tools. When these wore out, they had to be replaced, and this led to a collectible transition in 1979 sets. The old S puncheon had been deteriorating for years and its mark had become scarcely recognizable as a letter S. It was replaced with a much more distinct mintmark midway through 1979, with both varieties being known in Proof for each denomination. Both mintmarks are small enough that many collectors have difficulty telling them apart, yet these transitional varieties have captured their attention ever since.

The Type 2 or Clear S mintmark is scarcer across the board, having been introduced near the end of Proof coin production for 1979. It is actually scarcer than the certified population suggests, because owners are much more likely to submit Type 2 coins for grading. Again, *variety* or *subtype* is better nomenclature than *Type*, but Type is firmly entrenched in the literature.

3,554,806 Complete Sets Possible

Denomination	PF-68 Ultra Cameo		PF-69 Ultra Cameo	
	Cert. Population	Value	Cert. Population	Value
Cent	341		925	
Nickel	342		1,843	
Dime	290		1,756	
Quarter	346		1,984	
Half Dollar	499		2,712	
Dollar	737		4,782	
Complete Set		$60		$110

Original Price: $10

Uncertified Value: $9

Original Packaging: The coins were mounted in a red plastic insert that was fitted between an upper and lower casing of transparent plastic. These parts were set within a black plastic frame bearing on its lower border the words UNITED STATES PROOF SET in silver letters. The frame included a slot into which the transparent casing could be inserted for desktop display. A black cardboard box housed the assembled set, and the words "United States Proof Set • 1980" were printed on it in silver script.

This holder, while appearing superficially similar to that used for the several years previous, was smaller in width. The hole for the Anthony dollar was of suitable diameter, permitting this size reduction. This style of holder was used through 1982, after which time the suspension of dollar coinage prompted its retirement.

Commentary: Though a failure as a circulating coin, the popularity of the Anthony dollar with collectors maintained high sales for this year's Proof set. In addition, the numismatic market overall was very hot in 1980, as investors and speculators sought to dodge the effects of double-digit inflation by putting money into coins. This may have contributed to high Proof set sales in 1980.

Sharp-eyed collectors may be able to spot the scarce and desirable repunched mintmark variety found on some of the 1980-S Proof dollars. This is a nice premium variety, though a lack of sale records makes pricing them difficult.

Cameo and ultra cameo coins are the rule, rather than the exception, for this date. They are still scarce in the higher grades, the cents in particular being difficult to find with full red color and no spotting or tarnishing.

Collector's Notebook – 1980
Kennedy half dollar, reverse

The reverse of the Kennedy half dollar is a familiar sight for anyone who's seen a presidential address on television. It features a stylized rendition of the Great Seal of the United States. The design has been used since 1964, with only one break for the Bicentennial design. Proofs number in the many millions.

1981-S

UNITED STATES PROOF SET

UNITED STATES PROOF SET

4,063,083 Complete Sets Possible

Denomination	PF-68 Ultra Cameo		PF-69 Ultra Cameo	
	Cert. Population	Value	Cert. Population	Value
Cent	366		829	
Nickel	377		2,389	
Dime	320		2,760	
Quarter	399		2,931	
Half Dollar	585		3,929	
Dollar	890		6,019	
Type 1 or Filled S Sets		$60		$110

Included above

Denomination	PF-68 Ultra Cameo		PF-69 Ultra Cameo	
	Cert. Population	Value	Cert. Population	Value
Cent	267		110	
Nickel	170		491	
Dime	92		358	
Quarter	132		561	
Half Dollar	303		675	
Dollar	759		1,089	
Type 2 or Clear S Sets		$500		$900

Original Price: $11

Uncertified Value: $10 (Filled S); $375 (Clear S)

Original Packaging: The coins were mounted in a red plastic insert that was fitted between an upper and lower casing of transparent plastic. These parts were set within a black plastic frame bearing on its lower border the words UNITED STATES PROOF SET in silver letters. The frame included a slot into which the transparent casing could be inserted for desktop display. A black cardboard box housed the assembled set, and the words "United States Proof Set • 1981" were printed on it in silver script.

Commentary: When it was announced that no Anthony dollars would be produced for circulation in 1981, collectors boosted sales of the Mint's Proof and Uncirculated sets. The high mintage for this date has hurt it a bit in the secondary market, with uncertified coins bringing no more than issue price even after twenty years of creeping inflation.

The dime received sharpened hubs for 1981. The portrait was lowered in relief and its details sculpted more distinctly. The new reverse featured broader and crisper lettering, as well as a similar lowering of relief. These changes extended the useful life of the dies. While such economy had little bearing on Proof production, it was essential to the mass production of coins for circulation.

In a repeat of 1979, the S mintmark puncheon was once again replaced after showing signs of failure. The Type 1 or Filled S of 1981 is, in fact, the Type 2 Clear S of 1979 after it, too, had deteriorated, and the terminology used is often confusing to collectors. While the 1981 Type 1 S is symmetrical and shaped much like the numeral 8 when viewed without a glass, the Type 2 mintmark is irregular in shape, with projecting knobs at each end.

Once again, both styles of mintmark are known for all denominations. The Type 2 mintmark is quite a bit more rare than it was in 1979, as the premiums attached to it reflect. The certified population is a bit misleading because submitters are more inclined to have the rare variety certified. This is an important concept across the board, for, in all series, coins with higher values have a higher certified population compared to their field population.

1982-S

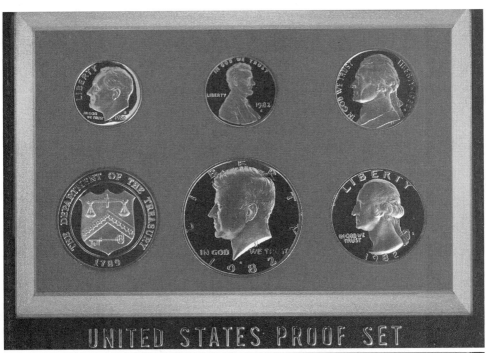

3,857,479 Complete Sets Possible

Denomination	PF-68 Ultra Cameo		PF-69 Ultra Cameo	
	Cert. Population	Value	Cert. Population	Value
Cent	87		669	
Nickel	92		1,223	
Dime	65		12,866	
Quarter	93		1,609	
Half Dollar	138		1,972	
Complete Set		$50		$75

Original Price: $11

Uncertified Value: $6

Original Packaging: The coins were mounted in a red plastic insert that was fitted between an upper and lower casing of transparent plastic. These parts were set within a black plastic frame bearing on its lower border the words UNITED STATES PROOF SET in silver letters. The frame included a slot into which the transparent casing could be inserted for desktop display. A black cardboard box housed the assembled set, and the words "United States Proof Set • 1982" were printed on it in silver script.

When no dollar coins were struck in 1982, the Mint was left with a large remaining stock of Proof set holders designed to fit the Anthony dollar. Rather than discard them at a loss, the Mint filled the dollar coin's hole with a bronze medal prepared from existing hubs. The obverse featured the familiar Treasury Department seal, while the reverse displayed the American eagle surrounded by the words UNITED STATES PROOF SET. Unique to 1982 Proof sets, this medal was itself coined in Proof.

Commentary: The high mintage of this year's Proof set is something of a mystery, as 1982 offered nothing special to the collector, save for the curious Proof medal that filled a vacancy left by the now-suspended Anthony dollar. In any case, this high mintage took its toll on the value of uncertified Proofs. This set is seemingly a bargain at current prices.

The composition of the cent was changed drastically midway through 1982 to address the rising price of copper. Though the new cents of zinc with a copper plating were produced for circulation alongside those of the traditional composition, all Proof cents of this date are of the 95% copper, 5% zinc alloy used in previous years. Also changed during the course of the 1982 regular coinage was the obverse hub of the cent, the new obverse having a portrait of slightly reduced size and a distinctly smaller date. All of the Proof cents, however, have the older style obverse with its large date.

Yet another S mintmark appeared in 1982, but it was not transitional, as it was used for all the Proofs of this date and through 1984. This mintmark featured distinct serifs at top and bottom.

Note: The Proof sets of 1978 and later years have a uniform cameo quality to them, with even deep or ultra cameo pieces being commonplace. Though the certified population data published by the major grading services may include non-cameo pieces, these were likely certified before the current language was adopted. It may be assumed that all such Proofs are cameo at the very least.

3,138,765 Complete Sets Possible

Denomination	PF-68 Ultra Cameo		PF-69 Ultra Cameo	
	Cert. Population	Value	Cert. Population	Value
Cent	96		915	
Nickel	88		1,272	
Dime	39		1,462	
Dime, No S	40		68	
Quarter	87		1,536	
Half Dollar	181		1,933	
Complete Set, Normal Dime		$50		$80
Complete Set, No S Dime		$800		$1,000

Original Price: $11

Uncertified Value: $7; $500 (No S dime)

Original Packaging: A transparent plastic casing with frosted borders surrounded a black plastic insert containing the coins. This was inserted into a blue cardboard box upon which the words "United States Proof Set • 1983" were printed in silver script.

The holder used from 1968 through 1972 was revived for 1983, the only difference being that the coins were mounted so that they faced what was formerly the back of the holder. This placed the embossed eagle above the half dollar's reverse instead of its obverse. The inscriptions "United States Mint Proof Set" and PACKAGED BY U.S. MINT thus moved from the back of the holder to its front.

Commentary: After the suspension of Susan B. Anthony dollar coinage, the U.S. Mint's Proof sets entered a period of repetition, in which each year's set looked much like the one before it. This had a steadily erosive effect on sales, with the nadir coming in the mid-1990s. The 1983-S Proof set was one of many that was purchased routinely each year by long-time customers on the Mint's mailing list.

The 1983-S Proof set included the new copper-plated zinc cents, which had become standard issue for circulation. Since the multiple strikings required for Proof coin production tended to break through the copper plating, exposing the underlying zinc, the Proof cents received a double coating of their copper plating. This remains standard practice to the present day for all Proof cents.

Once again, an obverse dime die was shipped to San Francisco without its S mintmark. The number of S-less Proof dimes distributed is unknown, but this variety appears to be more readily available than earlier Proof varieties for which the intended S mintmark was accidentally omitted.

The quarter dollar became the latest denomination to receive a reworking by the Mint's engraving department. This is most noticeable on the obverse, where the portrait was reduced slightly in relief as well as in overall size, with the lettering sharpened and moved inward from the borders.

To expand its sales and offer something distinctive to collectors, the U.S. Mint began marketing Prestige Proof sets in 1983. This year's set featured special packaging that enclosed not only the five regular Proofs but also the 1983-S Olympic silver dollar commemorative. Priced at a whopping $59, only 140,361 sets were sold.

Prestige Proof sets were offered for several commemorative issues as late as 1997, when this program was discontinued. Sold in relatively small numbers, they remain scarce and lie beyond the scope of this book. They will be mentioned in passing but not studied in detail.

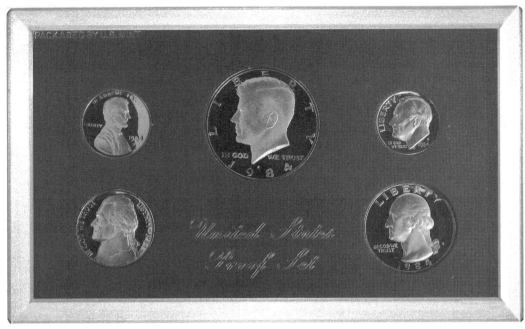

Denomination	PF-68 Ultra Cameo		PF-69 Ultra Cameo	
	Cert. Population	Value	Cert. Population	Value
Cent	60		128	
Nickel	86		1,289	
Dime	42		1,482	
Quarter	49		1,448	
Half Dollar	125		1,805	
Complete Set		$60		$90

Original Price: $11

Uncertified Value: $10

Original Packaging: The year's holder is similar to that of 1983, except as noted. A two-piece, transparent plastic with frosted borders held a purple fiberboard insert containing holes for the coins. This was slipped into a purple cardboard box upon which the words "United States Proof Set • 1984" were printed in silver script.

This format remained the Mint's standard packaging for Proof sets for the next decade.

Commentary: The 1984-S Proof set had a mintage significantly lower than in 1983. Since sales rebounded the following year, it may be considered a statistical blip and not reflective of any trend.

The relief of the cent was drastically lowered in several stages, beginning in 1984. On this year's cent, Lincoln's upper arm has been hollowed out, an effect that is readily apparent in a side-by-side comparison with the 1983 cent. This action was taken to eliminate a striking problem that had plagued the Memorial cent since its inception in 1959. The motto E PLURIBUS UNUM did not strike up fully on most cents made for general circulation because the height of Lincoln's shoulder, directly opposite this feature on the obverse, was too high to permit complete filling of the dies in a single blow from the press. Of course, this was not a problem with Proofs, which were struck two or three times, but the same master hub produced dies for both circulating coins and Proofs.

The Prestige Proof Set for 1984 included the 1984 edition of the Olympics silver dollar. It was offered at $59, and 316,680 sets were sold.

Collector's Notebook – 1984
Jefferson nickel, reverse

The reverse of the Jefferson nickel features the president's home, Monticello—the mansion masterpiece he designed, tinkered with, built, and rebuilt for more than 40 years. Proof mintages of two or three million coins per year have been common since the 1960s.

3,362,821 Complete Sets Possible

Denomination	PF-68 Ultra Cameo		PF-69 Ultra Cameo	
	Cert. Population	Value	Cert. Population	Value
Cent	72		1,605	
Nickel	66		1,578	
Dime	47		1,683	
Quarter	76		1,874	
Half Dollar	126		2,259	
Complete Set		$50		$90

Original Price: $11

Uncertified Value: $7

Original Packaging: A two-piece, transparent plastic casing with frosted borders held a purple fiberboard insert containing holes for the coins. This was slipped into a purple cardboard box upon which the words "United States Proof Set • 1985" were printed in silver script.

Commentary: The 1985 Proof set was a routine entry in the series that experienced typical sales and a fairly typical aftermarket value. By this time, that meant that its value fell soon after issue. This was a situation that did nothing to encourage new customers, but the established names on the Mint's mailing list continued to purchase predictable numbers of Proof sets each year, often as something to put away for the grandchildren.

A new style of S mintmark debuted in 1985 and continued in use for the next several years. 1985 was also the first year that the Mint began punching the S mintmark once into the master die for a particular coin type rather than punching it into each and every working die. This same procedure was used for each year through 1989, after which time the mintmark was simply included as a sculpted part of the design itself, eliminating the punching of mintmarks once and for all.

Ultra or deep cameo Proofs are the norm for 1985 sets, though preservation is sometimes an issue with these sets, for they have the fiberboard inserts typical of the time. Collectors complained early on that the coins were subject to acquiring a hazy film. Particularly problematic were the cents, with their highly reactive zinc base. The solution would have been to coin Proof cents in the traditional alloy of 95% copper, but this would have required special legislation that evidently was not sought by the Mint.

Collector's Notebook – 1985

Lincoln Memorial cent, reverse

Modern Proofs of the Lincoln cent are common and well struck, with quantities minted in the millions. The reverse design centers on the Lincoln Memorial found in Washington, D.C.—one of the most moving of the capital's many national monuments.

Denomination	PF-68 Ultra Cameo		PF-69 Ultra Cameo	
	Cert. Population	Value	Cert. Population	Value
Cent	91		1,610	
Nickel	90		1,580	
Dime	50		1,685	
Quarter	87		1,875	
Half Dollar	143		2,261	
Complete Set		$50		$90

Original Price: $11

Uncertified Value: $24

Original Packaging: A two-piece, transparent plastic casing with frosted borders held a purple fiberboard insert containing holes for the coins. This was slipped into a purple cardboard box upon which the words "United States Proof Set • 1986" were printed in silver script.

Commentary: Though the number of Proof sets sold in 1986 is only moderately smaller than for 1984, this set has enjoyed a premium value for some years now. While this supposed rarity may be more a matter of perception than reality, dealers will argue that in some years sets were more widely dispersed among a greater number of purchasers, making it harder to obtain marketable quantities. This seems to have been the case with the 1986 sets but, as the years go by and the original purchasers place their sets on the market, this situation should correct itself.

The Prestige Proof set for 1986 included the very popular Statue of Liberty half dollar and silver dollar. The price now lowered to $48.50, it sold an impressive 599,317 units.

Collector's Notebook – 1986

Statue of Liberty silver dollar, reverse

The design of this 100th anniversary commemorative is striking: on the obverse, the statue itself, along with the gateway to Ellis Island; and on the reverse, Liberty's hand bearing the torch of freedom in a blaze of Art Deco-esque light. More than 6.4 million Proofs were coined—among commemoratives, a figure topped only by the 6.9 million half dollars of the same year and commemoration.

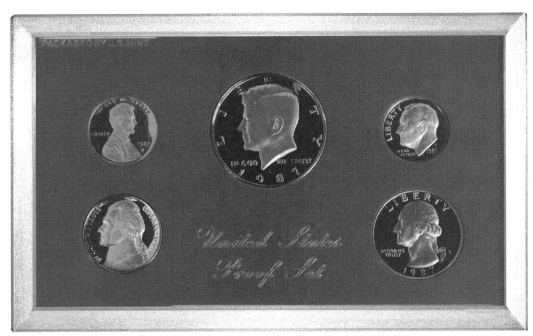

3,792,233 Complete Sets Possible

Denomination	PF-68 Ultra Cameo		PF-69 Ultra Cameo	
	Cert. Population	Value	Cert. Population	Value
Cent	126		1,037	
Nickel	87		1,539	
Dime	43		1,536	
Quarter	67		1,877	
Half Dollar	182		2,422	
Complete Set		$55		$90

Original Price: $11

Uncertified Value: $6

Original Packaging: A two-piece, transparent plastic casing with frosted borders held a purple fiberboard insert containing holes for the coins. This was slipped into a purple cardboard box upon which the words "United States Proof Set • 1987" were printed in silver script.

Commentary: 1987 is another routine entry in this long and popular series. There are no significant varieties or rarities to report.

Sales were up this year for a very simple reason. It was announced at the beginning of the year that no half dollars would be coined for circulation, so collectors scrambled to purchase extra Proof sets and Uncirculated sets. By 1987 it was clear to everyone that the half dollar was no longer a circulating coin and had not been one since the 1960s. The announcement of a one-year suspension in half dollar coinage for circulation was, in all likelihood, just a marketing gimmick on the part of the Mint to boost interest in its products.

Though sales of Proof sets had been fairly steady through the 1980s, interest in the Mint's Uncirculated sets was way down. The limited edition half dollars of 1987 caused a spike in the sales of both products, though it was just a temporary boost. The high sales resulted in a poor secondary market for this year's Proof set, and it is a much better buy today than it was in 1987.

The Prestige Proof set for 1987 included the Constitution Bicentennial silver dollar. Priced at $45, some 435,495 sets were sold.

Collector's Notebook – 1987

Constitution silver dollar, obverse

The surface of a coin may be the single best place to make a lasting statement; few other media are as durable or retain their original beauty almost indefinitely if properly cared for. The year 1987 marked the 200th anniversary of the U.S. Constitution, a document whose physical existence is preserved only by exacting techniques. Much more durable is any one of the 2.7 million Proofs commemorating the Constitution's anniversary—perhaps the only thing that can outlast them, in fact, is the spirit of the Constitution itself.

3,031,287 Complete Sets Possible

Denomination	PF-68 Ultra Cameo		PF-69 Ultra Cameo	
	Cert. Population	Value	Cert. Population	Value
Cent	51		1,305	
Nickel	63		1,071	
Dime	46		1,100	
Quarter	68		1,275	
Half Dollar	199		1,758	
Complete Set		$55		$90

Original Price: $11

Uncertified Value: $10

Original Packaging: A two-piece, transparent plastic casing with frosted borders held a purple fiberboard insert containing holes for the coins. This was slipped into a purple cardboard box upon which the words "United States Mint Proof Set • 1988" were printed in silver script.

Commentary: After the excitement of the 1987 limited edition half dollars, the sales of Proof sets settled down a bit in 1988. As is usually the case, a lessened interest at the time has resulted in better prices in the aftermarket.

As the 1980s progressed, the Mint accelerated its program of reducing the relief of circulating coins. Of course, these changes are evident in the Proofs, too, since the same master hubs produced dies for both issues. The half dollar, in particular, is noticeably different from 1987 to 1988. The changes made to its obverse are fairly subtle, but its reverse is in distinctly lower relief.

Unrelated to this change is a doubled-die obverse variety for the 1988-S Proof half dollar. Very slight, its doubling affects the word TRUST.

As with all Proof coins of the 1980s, the 1988 Proofs were made with deeply frosted legends and devices. While some of this frostiness may have eroded a bit as the dies wore, accounting for the simply "cameo" listings found among the certified population, lightly frosted coins were now the exception.

The Prestige Proof set for 1988 featured that year's Olympics silver dollar. 231,661 sets were sold at a price of $45.

In 1988 the San Francisco facility, which had been downgraded to "assay office" status in 1958, was finally given its due when Congress officially restored its title as the San Francisco Mint.

Collector's Notebook – 1988
24th Olympiad silver dollar, reverse

The 1988 Olympics were held in Seoul, South Korea, where athletes pursued some 241 gold medals, 234 silver medals, and 264 bronze medals. Collectors, irrespective of athletic prowess, have been able to pursue almost 1.4 million silver Proofs coined to commemorate the 24th Olympiad.

3,009,107 Complete Sets Possible

Denomination	PF- 69 Ultra Cameo	
	Cert. Population	Value
Cent	1,353	
Nickel	1,192	
Dime	1,056	
Quarter	1,258	
Half Dollar	1,675	
Complete Set		$100

Original Price: $11

Uncertified Value: $10

Original Packaging: A two-piece, transparent plastic casing with frosted borders held a purple fiberboard insert containing holes for the coins. This was slipped into a purple cardboard box upon which the words "United States Mint Proof Set • 1989" were printed in silver script.

Commentary: The 1989-S Proof set was a near twin of its immediate predecessor, priced the same at issue and with a very similar mintage. Why its value is currently a bit higher is one of the puzzles that make collecting of Proof sets so interesting.

1989 was the last year in which our Proof coins bore mintmarks that were actually hand punched into a die. Though this punching had been performed solely on the master die since 1985, resulting in no varieties or positional changes of any kind, it did lend a certain human element to the coins that has been lacking ever since.

The clad half dollar and the silver dollar issued to commemorate the bicentennial of Congress were featured in the 1989 Prestige Proof set. Priced at $45, a somewhat disappointing 211,087 units were sold by the Mint. Despite the rarity of such sets, collectors do not seem to be drawn to them today, and most are selling below issue price. Should an interest in this series develop, Prestige Proof sets may prove to be very elusive.

Collector's Notebook – 1989
Congress silver dollar, obverse

The mintage of Proof silver dollars honoring the 200th anniversary of the U.S. Congress—762,198—was about par for commemoratives in general. Above par, however, is the obverse design: the Statue of Freedom against a background of clouds and rays of light, designed by muralist William Woodward.

2,793,433 Complete Sets Possible

Denomination	PF-69 Ultra Cameo	
	Cert. Population	Value
Cent	1,951	
Cent, No S	2,047	
Nickel	1,911	
Dime	1,911	
Quarter	2,162	
Half Dollar	2,591	
Complete Set, Normal Cent		$100
Complete Set, No S Cent		$10,000

Original Price: $11

Uncertified Value: $10; $7,000 (No S Cent)

Original Packaging: A two-piece, transparent plastic casing with frosted borders held a purple fiberboard insert containing holes for the coins. This was slipped into a purple cardboard box upon which the words "United States Mint Proof Set • 1990" were printed in silver script.

Commentary: Sales of Proof sets were down from 1989, and once again that has resulted in greater value in the secondary market.

The big story for 1990 was the S-less Proof cent. The cause of this error was the same as for previous Proof coins lacking their mintmark—it was simply omitted from the die when sent by the Philadelphia Mint. The number of these coins the Mint says was issued is 3,555, but the great rarity of this variety as compared to the other No S varieties suggests that the actual number is lower. 1990 is recent enough that many original purchasers of S-less sets may still have them sitting undetected, so more examples may yet turn up. A few of these error cents have been reported with the Prestige Proof sets for 1990.

Beginning this year, the Mint ceased to punch mintmarks into any of the Proof master dies, instead sculpting them as an integral part of a separate model from which master hubs and dies were reduced mechanically. The exact procedure involved is beyond the scope of this book, but what is important is the effect it had on variety collecting. No longer would there be repunched mintmarks, such as D D or D S. Furthermore, any die doubling that occurred would affect the mintmark too. Validation of this was not long in coming, as a few of the Proof quarters dated 1990 feature a doubled-die obverse in which the mintmark itself is boldly doubled!

The 1990 Prestige Proof set included the handsome silver dollar honoring the centennial of Dwight D. Eisenhower's birth. Some 506,126 sets were sold at $45 apiece, these higher than usual sales reflecting both the popularity of the subject matter and the attractiveness of the coin itself.

2,610,833 Complete Sets Possible

Denomination	PF-69 Ultra Cameo	
	Cert. Population	Value
Cent	1,438	
Nickel	1,360	
Dime	1,211	
Quarter	1,489	
Half Dollar	1,935	
Complete Set		$110

Original Price: $11

Uncertified Value: $16

Original Packaging: A two-piece, transparent plastic casing with frosted borders held a purple fiberboard insert containing holes for the coins. This was slipped into a purple cardboard box upon which the words "United States Mint Proof Set • 1991" were printed in silver script.

Commentary: Sales of regular Proof sets declined again in 1991, as the generation that remembered the exciting Proof set market of the 1950s and '60s began to pass. When interest revived during the late 1990s, sets such as this one received greater attention, and now command good premiums over their issue price.

The relief of all United States coins continued to be lowered during the early 1990s. While this was done to address die-life issues relating to the circulating coinage, its depressing effect on the sculptural quality of the coins is most painfully evident in the Proofs. While richly detailed, United States coins of recent years seem almost two-dimensional and lack the boldness they possessed when each respective design was new.

The 1991 Prestige Proof set included the clad half dollar and silver dollar honoring the golden anniversary of South Dakota's Mount Rushmore Memorial. Some 256,954 sets were sold at $59 apiece, and they are seldom seen in the aftermarket.

Collector's Notebook – 1991

Mount Rushmore half dollar, obverse

While the Mount Rushmore monument itself remains controversial, the presidents it honors—Washington, Jefferson, Roosevelt, and Lincoln—are not. Half of the surcharges from the sale of the 753,257 silver Proofs went to the Mount Rushmore National Memorial Society of Black Hills, SD, for the upkeep of the famous faces.

1992-S CLAD PROOF SET

2,675,618 Complete Sets Possible

Denomination	PF-69 Ultra Cameo	
	Cert. Population	Value
Cent	2,716	
Nickel	2,559	
Dime	1,251	
Quarter	1,441	
Half Dollar	1,616	
Complete Clad Proof Set		$100

Original Price: $11

Uncertified Value: $8

Original Packaging: A two-piece, transparent plastic casing with frosted borders held a purple fiberboard insert containing holes for the coins. This was slipped into a purple cardboard box upon which the words "United States Mint Proof Set • 1992" were printed in silver script.

NOTE: It should be mentioned that the U.S. Mint's Proof sets each included a Certificate of Authenticity and Specifications sheet printed on cardboard. These were tucked into each box containing the assembled sets. Their contents varied from time to time, so a complete description of them is not included in this study, but they are a standard component of all subsequent sets.

Commentary: Sales of the regular Proof set were about the same as in 1991, seemingly unaffected by collector interest in the silver Proof sets. In keeping with a general trend affecting all Proof sets of the 1990s, this issue is now worth somewhat more than its original price from the Mint. This probably reflects a greater focus by collectors on recent coinage than it does the actual rarity of the sets.

Several denominations were visibly modified for 1992. Beginning this year and continuing thereafter, Lincoln now reveals a bulging vein on his forehead. Washington has deeply incised hairlines on his periwig, and his cheeks seem a bit hollow. President Kennedy has a clearly defined part to his hair; the Mint's engravers evidently did not realize that this feature was deliberately omitted in 1964 at the request of Mrs. Kennedy.

Like all United States Proof sets of the 1980s and later, each coin features deeply frosted lettering and devices. Proof sets of this era are nearly perfect as made, though examination with a magnifying glass may reveal minute flaws such as tiny bright spots within the frosting.

1992 Prestige Proof sets included the clad half dollar and silver dollar minted for that year's Olympic games. At $56 a set, sales were a disappointing 183,293 units.

Collector's Notebook – 1992
25th Olympiad silver dollar (baseball), obverse

In 1992 the collector could introduce both nostalgia and history to his collection with this coin featuring one of America's best-known cultural images: a baseball pitcher winding up for the perfect throw. The number of Proof coins struck surpasses just over half a million.

1992-S SILVER PROOF SET

1,009,586 Complete Sets Possible

Denomination	PF-69 Ultra Cameo	
	Cert. Population	Value
Cent	Listed under 1992-S clad set	
Nickel	Listed under 1992-S clad set	
Dime	1,543	
Quarter	1,637	
Half Dollar	1,920	
Complete Silver Proof Set		$150

Original Price: $21

Uncertified Value: $18

Original Packaging: A two-piece, transparent plastic casing with frosted borders held a black fiberboard insert containing holes for the coins. Printed on this insert was the word "Silver" in silver script. The assembled set was slipped into a black cardboard box upon which the words "United States Mint Silver Proof Set • 1992" were printed in silver script.

The plastic components of this set's holder were identical to those used for the regular Proof set, and only the paper elements differed, as described above.

Commentary: Collectors clamored for special coins honoring the U.S. Mint's bicentennial in 1992, but a commemorative medal was struck instead. One consolation was that additional Proof sets were offered in which the three coins historically stuck in 90% silver—the dime, quarter, and half dollar—were again made available in that composition. It was not clear at the time whether this program would continue after the bicentennial year, but collector response was sufficient that the Mint did indeed make silver Proof sets a regular part of its line of collectors' coins. They are still being offered to the present day.

Also offered in 1992 was the new silver Premier Proof set. This consisted of the same five coins in deluxe packaging, and it was priced at $37 per set. Premier Proof sets are not to be confused with Prestige Proof Sets, which include one or more commemorative coins in addition to the regular types.

Because the cent and nickel were of the same composition in both the regular and silver Proof sets, this led to a curious situation not experienced since the Proof sets of 1975 and 1976. Collectors who purchase both the regular and silver Proof editions, and then break up the sets, find themselves with duplicate cents and nickels. Note how the certified populations of these two coins have risen beginning with 1992.

A slight doubled-die obverse variety may be found for the 1992-S silver half dollar. The doubling is just barely detectable in the word TRUST.

The quality of the Mint's silver Proof coins has been superb since the outset of this program in 1992, and the greater brilliance of silver makes their ultra cameo contrast all the more dramatic.

1993-S CLAD PROOF SET

| Denomination | PF-69 Ultra Cameo | |
	Cert. Population	Value
Cent	2,164	
Nickel	2,130	
Dime	1,066	
Quarter	1,525	
Half Dollar	1,457	
Complete Clad Proof Set		$100

Original Price: $12.50

Uncertified Value: $16

Original Packaging: A two-piece, transparent plastic casing with frosted borders held a purple fiberboard insert containing holes for the coins. This was slipped into a purple cardboard box upon which the words "United States Mint Proof Set • 1993" were printed in silver script.

Commentary: The issue price of this year's set rose from previous years, but this seems to have had no impact on sales. Typical of Proof sets from the 1990s, the 1993 regular Proof set has held its value well.

Included within the 1993 Prestige Proof set were the clad half dollar and silver dollar honoring the bicentennial of the Bill of Rights. Since that anniversary actually occurred in 1991, less emphasis was placed on this theme in the actual designs, which are better known for portraying the bill's author, James Madison. Some 224,045 sets were sold at $57 apiece.

Collector's Notebook – 1993

James Madison half dollar, obverse

Collectors could add the father of the Bill of Rights to their collections quite easily by obtaining this commemorative—more than half a million Proof coins were struck. The 1993 James Madison half dollar honors America's fourth president; he sits, quill-pen in hand, before the Bill of Rights, steadily writing America's most beloved freedoms.

1993 SILVER PROOF SET

Denomination	PF-69 Ultra Cameo	
	Cert. Population	Value
Cent	Listed under 1993-S clad set	
Nickel	Listed under 1993-S clad set	
Dime	1,142	
Quarter	1,104	
Half Dollar	1,373	
Complete Silver Proof Set		$125

Original Price: $21

Uncertified Value: $42

Original Packaging: A two-piece, transparent plastic casing with frosted borders held a black fiberboard insert containing holes for the coins. Printed on this insert was the word "Silver" in silver script. The assembled set was slipped into a black cardboard box upon which the words "United States Mint Silver Proof Set • 1993" were printed in silver script.

Commentary: With the Mint's bicentennial over, far fewer of the silver Proof sets were sold in 1993. The scarcity and popularity of this edition are reflected in the solid after market price.

The silver Premier Proof set was again offered this year, selling a mere 191,140 units. For some reason not revealed, its price was raised just 50¢ to $37.50.

Collector's Notebook – 1993

Jefferson silver dollar, obverse

The birth of Thomas Jefferson was celebrated in 1993 with a silver dollar commemorative. The coin bears the portrait of a handsome young Jefferson on the obverse, and a finely detailed depiction of Monticello on the reverse. Proofs number 332,891.

2,308,701 Complete Sets Possible

Denomination	PF-69 Ultra Cameo	
	Cert. Population	Value
Cent	2,130	
Nickel	2,077	
Dime	1,043	
Quarter	1,124	
Half Dollar	1,328	
Complete Clad Proof Set		$110

Original Price: $12.50

Uncertified Value: $22

Original Packaging: A two-piece, transparent plastic casing with frosted borders held a green fiberboard insert containing holes for the coins. This was slipped into a green cardboard box upon which the words "United States Mint Proof Set • 1994" were printed in silver script.

Commentary: The Mint's traditional offering of the regular Proof set resulted in modest sales that were fairly typical of this period. Interest in current or recent coinage was very low at this time, entirely unlike the heated market that developed in the late 1990s and continues to the present day.

The Prestige Proof set for 1994 included the clad half dollar and silver dollar honoring the USA's hosting of the World Cup games. Like Americans' interest in soccer, sales were limited, with only 175,893 sets delivered at $57 apiece.

Collector's Notebook – 1994
World Cup silver dollar, obverse

The U.S. Mint made a coin for America and a coin for the world with its 1994 World Cup silver dollar, with Proof mintages approaching 600,000. Featuring two competing soccer players battling for the ball, the coin represents America's turn as host of the tournament that unites nations in friendly competitive sportsmanship.

1994-S SILVER PROOF SET

Denomination	PF-69 Ultra Cameo	
	Cert. Population	Value
Cent	Listed under 1994-S clad set	
Nickel	Listed under 1994-S clad set	
Dime	1,041	
Quarter	973	
Half Dollar	1,208	
Complete Silver Proof Set		$150

Original Price: $21

Uncertified Value: $50

Original Packaging: A two-piece, transparent plastic casing with frosted borders held a black fiberboard insert containing holes for the coins. Printed on this insert was the word "Silver" in silver script. The assembled set was slipped into a black cardboard box upon which the words "United States Mint Silver Proof Set • 1994" were printed in silver script.

Commentary: It appears that a pattern of sales had already developed by 1994, with the mintage of this year's set fairly similar to that of the 1993 offering. The level of interest shown in these coins at the time clearly did not give any indication of their later popularity.

The Premier Proof set saw its sales decline to just 149,320 units. The coins in this set are duplicates of those in the $21 set, so it is only the packaging that is unique. As many collectors are inclined to seek coins that have been broken out of their original packaging and certified by third-party grading services, the market for specially packaged products of the U.S. Mint is currently limited. Should the emphasis ever change, these distinctive packaging options may prove to be quite scarce.

Collector's Notebook – 1994

Vietnam Memorial silver dollar, reverse

Collectors can honor the soldiers of the Vietnam War with this commemorative coin featuring and marking the 10th anniversary of the Vietnam Veterans Memorial in Washington, D.C. Proof strikes number 226,262.

1995-S CLAD PROOF SET

2,010,384 Complete Sets Possible

Denomination	PF-69 Ultra Cameo	
	Cert. Population	Value
Cent	1,859	
Nickel	1,739	
Dime	735	
Quarter	844	
Half Dollar	967	
Complete Clad Proof Set		$225

Original Price: $12.50

Uncertified Value: $80

Original Packaging: A two-piece, transparent plastic casing with frosted borders held a green fiberboard insert containing holes for the coins. This was slipped into a green cardboard box upon which the words "United States Mint Proof Set • 1995" were printed in silver script.

Commentary: Sales of this year's regular Proof set were remarkably low, but there was a reason for this. The commemorative coin program for the Atlanta Olympiad was so extensive that it left collectors either too tapped out to purchase their usual extra Proof sets or simply too frustrated or exhausted to care. This same situation was in effect the following year, when Proof set sales declined even further.

The Prestige Proof set for 1995 included the clad half dollar and silver dollar issued to honor Civil War battlefield preservation. With collectors' budgets strained by the Olympic program, a mere 107,112 sets were sold at $57 per set.

Collector's Notebook – 1995
Civil War Battlefields silver dollar, obverse

The Civil War Battlefield Preservation silver dollar is a handsome coin representing history, bravery, and the human spirit. The Proof coin collector who seeks this more human image of liberty will need to search among the strikes that number 327,686.

549,878 Complete Sets Possible

Denomination	PF-69 Ultra Cameo	
	Cert. Population	Value
Cent	Listed under 1995-S clad set	
Nickel	Listed under 1995-S clad set	
Dime	1,087	
Quarter	1,072	
Half Dollar	1,217	
Complete Silver Proof Set		$275

Original Price: $21

Uncertified Value: $125

Original Packaging: A two-piece, transparent plastic casing with frosted borders held a black fiberboard insert containing holes for the coins. Printed on this insert was the word "Silver" in silver script. The assembled set was slipped into a black cardboard box upon which the words "United States Mint Silver Proof Set • 1995" were printed in silver script.

Commentary: Another winning edition for collectors, those who made an effort to acquire this set from the Mint were handsomely rewarded. Sales were down from the previous year, and these coins are relatively scarce.

The silver Premier Proof set is another modern rarity, with just 130,107 sets sold. Again, the likely explanation is that collectors simply had to decide between the many Olympic coins offered and these routine offerings. It appears that most decided to overlook this set, which was now in its fourth year.

Collector's Notebook – 1995

Silver Eagle, reverse

The lowest mintage for a Proof Silver Eagle bullion coin is that of the 1995 West Point striking. Only 30,125 pieces were made, leading to premiums of several thousand dollars for a bullion item whose worth is theoretically tied only to the value of an ounce of silver.

1996-S CLAD PROOF SET

1,695,244 Complete Sets Possible

Denomination	PF-69 Ultra Cameo	
	Cert. Population	Value
Cent	1,883	
Nickel	1,859	
Dime	866	
Quarter	1,100	
Half Dollar	1,087	
Complete Clad Proof Set		$100

Original Price: $12.50

Uncertified Value: $18

Original Packaging: A two-piece, transparent plastic casing with frosted borders held a green fiberboard insert containing holes for the coins. This was slipped into a green cardboard box upon which the words "United States Mint Proof Set • 1996" were printed in silver script.

Commentary: Not since 1960 had there been a regular Proof set with such a modest mintage! Interest in these sets was perhaps at an all-time low, as they competed with silver Proof sets, commemorative coins, and American Eagle bullion coins for the collector's disposable income. While the current value of uncertified 1996 sets is surprisingly low, it is likely that this set will prove to be a winner in the long run.

This year's Prestige Proof set featured one clad half dollar and one silver dollar from among the several issues of the 1996 Olympiad. This set had a shockingly low mintage of only 55,000 units sold! As noted for the Premier Proof sets, however, the coins themselves were available in much larger numbers, and it is only the unique packaging option that is rare. Should a broader market for these rare variants ever emerge, this set will become a highly sought item.

Collector's Notebook – 1996
Smithsonian Institution silver dollar, reverse

The collector of modern Proof coins might add to his storehouse this lofty silver dollar, struck to commemorate the Smithsonian Institution's dedication to "the increase and diffusion of knowledge." Slightly more than 126,000 were struck—a typical quantity for Proof silver dollars of the time.

1996-S SILVER PROOF SET

Denomination	PF-69 Ultra Cameo	
	Cert. Population	Value
Cent	Listed under 1996-S clad set	
Nickel	Listed under 1996-S clad set	
Dime	1,081	
Quarter	1,036	
Half Dollar	1,182	
Complete Silver Proof Set		$200

Original Price: $21

Uncertified Value: $60

Original Packaging: A two-piece, transparent plastic casing with frosted borders held a black fiberboard insert containing holes for the coins. Printed on this insert was the word "Silver" in silver script. The assembled set was slipped into a black cardboard box upon which the words "United States Mint Silver Proof Set • 1996" were printed in silver script.

Commentary: The 1996-S silver Proof set enjoyed typical sales for the period and is not especially rare. The quality of the coins, needless to say, is nearly perfect. The majority of certified examples grade Proof-68 ultra cameo and higher, yet these top-grade coins enjoy a strong following among the current generation of collectors.

Sales of the silver Premier Proof set were fairly close to those of 1995, some 151,366 sets being placed with happy buyers.

Collector's Notebook – 1996
Smithsonian $5 gold, reverse

Fewer than 22,000 numismatists will be lucky enough to add this Proof $5 gold commemorative to their collections. Those who do, however, should beware the coin's tendency toward hairline scratches in the central field of the sundial on the reverse. The coin honors James Smithson, the British scientist who left his fortune to the people of the United States, giving birth to the Smithsonian Institution.

1997-S CLAD PROOF SET

Denomination	PF-69 Ultra Cameo	
	Cert. Population	Value
Cent	1,549	
Nickel	1,745	
Dime	762	
Quarter	901	
Half Dollar	967	
Complete Clad Proof Set		$225

Original Price: $12.50

Uncertified Value: $60

Original Packaging: A two-piece, transparent plastic casing with frosted borders held a green fiberboard insert containing holes for the coins. This was slipped into a green cardboard box upon which the words "United States Mint Proof Set • 1997" were printed in silver script.

Commentary: The 1997 regular Proof set was another one that enjoyed a fairly low mintage, though the numbers sold rebounded from 1996's low. Perhaps the amazingly low sales the year before prompted more purchases in 1997. In any case, this set remains consistently popular and in demand.

The long-ailing Prestige Proof set concept was now in its final year, and the 1997 edition included the silver dollar honoring the National Botanic Garden in Washington, D.C. While a mere 80,000 units were reportedly sold, researchers are aware that the Mint's records of sales for recent years are incomplete and sometimes contradictory, so it is not certain whether these sets are truly that rare. A reliable accounting of sales might never be made.

Collector's Notebook – 1997
Botanic Garden silver dollar, obverse

Coin-collecting gardeners were granted a rare treat in 1997: the first modern United States commemorative to feature a plant (a rose in bloom) as its central design motif. Almost 265,000 Proofs were struck, honoring the United States Botanic Garden established by Congress in 1820.

1997-S SILVER PROOF SET

605,473 Complete Sets Possible

Denomination	PF-69 Ultra Cameo	
	Cert. Population	Value
Cent	Listed under 1997-S clad set	
Nickel	Listed under 1997-S clad set	
Dime	982	
Quarter	974	
Half Dollar	1,120	
Complete Silver Proof Set		$300

Original Price: $21

Uncertified Value: $110

Original Packaging: A two-piece, transparent plastic casing with frosted borders held a black fiberboard insert containing holes for the coins. Printed on this insert was the word "Silver" in silver script. The assembled set was slipped into a black cardboard box upon which the words "United States Mint Silver Proof Set • 1997" were printed in silver script.

Commentary: A modest but fairly typical mintage was recorded for the 1997 silver Proof sets. These are in constant demand, as is true for nearly all Proof sets of the 1990s.

Offered this year at $37.50 per set, the silver Premier Proof set was nearing the end of its days. Some 136,205 sets were sold for 1997, and these remain quite scarce.

Collector's Notebook – 1997
Jackie Robinson silver dollar, obverse

Fans of two of America's great pastimes—baseball and coin collecting—were pleased to see this 1997 commemorative honoring Jackie Robinson's contributions to the sport and to U.S. history. The silver dollar saw just over 110,000 pieces struck in Proof, to accompany about a quarter that number struck for the $5 gold coin in the same series. The Mint State version of the $5 gold is the true rarity, however, with a mere 5,174 pieces struck.

2,086,507 Complete Sets Possible

Denomination	Proof 69 Ultra Cameo	
	Cert. Population	Value
Cent	1,671	
Nickel	1,401	
Dime	738	
Quarter	873	
Half Dollar	982	
Complete Clad Proof Set		$220

Original Price: $12.50

Uncertified Value: $35

Original Packaging: A two-piece, transparent plastic casing with frosted borders held a green fiberboard insert containing holes for the coins. This was slipped into a green cardboard box upon which the words "United States Mint Proof Set • 1998" were printed in silver script.

Commentary: 1998 witnessed another low mintage for the regular Proof set. It was a bit higher than in 1997, perhaps because an announcement of the impending 50 State Quarters® Program sparked some additional interest. This set remains scarce and popular in the secondary market, as its high value suggests.

The Prestige Proof set was now a thing of the past, and none were offered in this and subsequent years.

Collector's Notebook – 1998
Robert F. Kennedy silver dollar, obverse

A little more than 99,000 examples of this commemorative silver dollar were struck in 1998. They honor Robert F. Kennedy, the U.S. Attorney General who was later elected Senator from New York. Eulogized after his assassination in 1968, Robert Kennedy was called by his brother Edward, "a good decent man, who saw wrong and tried to right it, saw suffering and tried to heal it, saw war and tried to stop it."

1998-S SILVER PROOF SET

Denomination	PF-69 Ultra Cameo	
	Cert. Population	Value
Cent	Listed under 1998-S clad set	
Nickel	Listed under 1998-S clad set	
Dime	1,093	
Quarter	1,146	
Half Dollar	1,239	
Complete Silver Proof Set		$200

Original Price: $21

Uncertified Value: $55

Original Packaging: A two-piece, transparent plastic casing with frosted borders held a black fiberboard insert containing holes for the coins. Printed on this insert was the word "Silver" in silver script. The assembled set was slipped into a black cardboard box upon which the words "United States Mint Silver Proof Set • 1998" were printed in silver script.

Commentary: As with the regular Proof set, sales of the silver edition crept up a bit from the previous year. This remains a very popular set, containing, as it does, what may prove to be the final Washington quarter with the old Flanagan reverse.

The silver Premier Proof set was offered for the final time this year, and it sold a respectable 240,658 units.

Collector's Notebook – 1998
Black Patriots silver dollar, obverse

This 1998 commemorative is regularly found in the highest state of Proof quality. Just over 75,000 pieces were struck, honoring the memory of Crispus Attucks (killed during the Boston Massacre of 1770) and all Black patriots of the American Revolution.

2,543,401 Nine-Piece Sets; 1,169,958 Five-Piece Sets

Denomination	PF-69 Ultra Cameo	
	Cert. Population	Value
Cent	4,485	
Nickel	4,834	
Dime	2,281	
Half Dollar	2,791	
Delaware Quarter	5,776	
Pennsylvannia Quarter	5,762	
New Jersey Quarter	5,809	
Georgia Quarter	5,796	
Connecticut Quarter	5,728	
Complete Clad Proof Set		$250

Original Price: $19.95 nine-piece set; $13.95 five-piece set

Uncertified Value: $80 nine-piece set; $75 five-piece set

Original Packaging: Two similar holders were required to house the nine coins in 1999's complete Proof set, and they differed only in their inserts and the selection of coins included. Each holder consisted of a two-piece, transparent plastic casing with frosted borders. This held a blue fiberboard insert featuring a background graphic of the American flag and holed appropriately for the coins it contained. One holder housed the cent, nickel, dime, and half dollar, while the other contained the five statehood quarters for 1999. The two holders were stacked and slipped into a flimsy, white cardboard box. This box was printed primarily in blue and featured a head view of the famous Statue of Liberty ("Liberty Enlightening the World"), along with starred upper and lower borders, the U.S. Mint's 50 State Quarters® logo, and the words UNITED STATES MINT PROOF SET 1999. The latter two elements both carry trademark symbols. On the reverse is the Treasury Department logo in white against the blue flag backdrop.

This packaging has been used for all subsequent regular Proof sets to date.

The five-piece sets consisted solely of the statehood quarters in copper-nickel clad composition. The holder for this set was simply one of the two holders comprising the complete set described above. Its packaging was similar to that of the complete sets, the primary difference being that an eagle appears on the outside of the box in place of the Statue of Liberty.

Commentary: While the cent, nickel, dime, and half dollar retained their pre-1999 designs, the quarter dollar was selected to host themes reflective of the 50 United States, each state being honored in the order that it joined the Union. Five state issues per year are minted, and the entire program is thus scheduled to last through 2008. With some of the U.S. territories also clamoring for their own issues, this program may yet be extended.

To accommodate the state themes, all statutory inscriptions have been moved to the obverse of the quarter. The bust of Washington was reduced to fit them in, and this modified bust now carries the initials of both its original designer, John Flanagan, and the U.S. Mint sculptor-engraver who adapted it, William Cousins.

The 50 State Quarters® Program has prompted a considerable revival of interest in coin collecting, bringing new participants into what had been an aging hobby population. Of course, interest among the newer collectors is heavily focused on recent-date coins, and this has driven up prices for many issues of the 1970s and later, which were formerly ignored.

The 1999-S Proof set was offered in two options. The nine-piece set included the four coins whose designs had not changed, as well as the five state quarters for this year. The clad Proof quarters alone could be purchased as a five-piece set, though most collectors seem to have favored complete sets. The revived Anthony dollar was not minted until the final quarter of 1999, so it came too late to be included in the sets. Proofs of the dollar were minted at Philadelphia and sold separately.

Despite having to perfect five entirely new coin reverses each year, the Mint has managed to maintain a fairly consistent quality throughout the state quarter period. While designs with more relief area naturally seem to be more frosty, there is actually little variation in the quality of the coins and their finishes.

804,565 Complete Sets Possible

Denomination	PF-69 Ultra Cameo	
	Cert. Population	Value
Cent	Listed under 1999-S clad set	
Nickel	Listed under 1999-S clad set	
Dime	2,461	
Half Dollar	3,652	
Delaware Quarter	7,085	
Pennsylvannia Quarter	6,840	
New Jersey Quarter	6,888	
Georgia Quarter	6,961	
Connecticut Quarter	6,905	
Complete Silver Proof Set		$400

Original Price: $31.95

Uncertified Value: $300

Original Packaging: Two holders were required to house all nine coins. Each holder consisted of a two-piece, transparent plastic casing with frosted borders. This held a red fiberboard insert labeled "Silver," featuring a background graphic of the American flag and holed appropriately for the coins it contained. One holder housed the cent, nickel, dime, and half dollar, while the other contained the five statehood quarters for 1999. The two holders were stacked and slipped into a white cardboard box. This box was printed primarily in red and featured a head shot of the famous Statue of Liberty ("Liberty Enlightening the World"), along with starred upper and lower borders, the U.S. Mint's 50 State Quarters® logo, and the words UNITED STATES MINT PROOF SET 1999. On the reverse is the Treasury Department logo in white against the red flag backdrop.

The packaging for the silver Proof set of 1999 was the same as for the regular sets, differing only in the color scheme of its paper components. This packaging has been used for all subsequent silver Proof sets to date.

Commentary: Not surprisingly, sales of the silver Proof set rose dramatically in 1999, as collectors eagerly sought the new state quarters in silver. Despite this higher mintage, the demand for both Mint-sealed sets and third-party certified singles and sets remains quite high.

Collector's Notebook – 1999
Dolley Madison silver dollar, obverse

This attractive silver dollar was minted to the tune of almost 225,000 pieces in Proof. It marks the first appearance of a First Lady on a U.S. commemorative: Dolley Madison, who famously rescued treasures from the White House when the British burned the mansion in 1814.

3,082,483 Ten-Piece Sets; 937,600 Five-Piece Set

Denomination	PF-69 Ultra Cameo	
	Cert. Population	Value
Cent	3,501	
Nickel	4,245	
Dime	1,355	
Half Dollar	1,991	
Dollar	7,827	
Massachusetts Quarter	5,020	
Maryland Quarter	4,861	
South Carolina Quarter	4,810	
New Hampshire Quarter	4,894	
Virginia Quarter	4,872	
Complete Clad Proof Set		$200

Original Price: $19.95 ten-piece set; $13.95 five-piece set

Uncertified Value: $25 ten-piece set; $18 five-piece set

Original Packaging: Two similar holders were required to house the ten coins in 2000's Proof set, and they differed only in their inserts and the selection of coins included. Each holder consisted of a two-piece, transparent plastic casing with frosted borders. This held a blue fiberboard insert featuring a background graphic of the American flag and holed appropriately for the coins it contained. One holder housed the cent, nickel, dime, half dollar, and dollar, while the other contained the five statehood quarters for 2000. The two holders were stacked and slipped into a white cardboard box. This box was printed primarily in blue and featured a head shot of the famous Statue of Liberty, along with starred upper and lower borders, the U.S. Mint's 50 State Quarters® logo, and the words UNITED STATES MINT PROOF SET 2000.

The five-piece sets consisted solely of the statehood quarters in copper-nickel clad composition. The holder for this set was simply one of the two holders comprising the complete set described above. An eagle appears on the box cover in place of the Statue of Liberty.

Commentary: The popularity of the 50 State Quarters® Program was reaffirmed in 2000 with impressive sales of the regular Proof set. This year's complete set included the new Sacagawea dollar, which served to further interest and sales. This coin actually leads the pack in the number of examples certified by third-party grading services.

Collector's Notebook – 2000
Library of Congress silver dollar, obverse

A mintage of up to 500,000 silver dollars was authorized to honor the bicentennial of the Library of Congress, founded in 1800. High-grade Proofs are readily available today, even in the highest levels of quality, PF-69 and PF-70.

2000-S SILVER PROOF SET

965,421 Complete Sets Possible

Denomination	PF-69 Ultra Cameo	
	Cert. Population	Value
Cent	Listed under 2000-S clad set	
Nickel	Listed under 2000-S clad set	
Dime	3,107	
Half Dollar	4,254	
Dollar	Listed under 2000-S clad set	
Massachusetts Quarter	6,572	
Maryland Quarter	6,403	
South Carolina Quarter	6,283	
New Hampshire Quarter	6,378	
Virginia Quarter	6,475	
Complete Silver Proof Set		$250

Original Price: $31.95

Uncertified Value: $40

Original Packaging: Two holders were required to house the ten coins. Each holder consisted of a two-piece, transparent plastic casing with frosted borders. This held a red fiberboard insert labeled "Silver," featuring a background graphic of the American flag and holed appropriately for the coins it contained. One holder housed the cent, nickel, dime, half dollar, and dollar, while the other contained the five statehood quarters for 2000. The two holders were stacked and slipped into a white cardboard box. This box was printed primarily in red and featured a head view of the famous statue Statue of Liberty, along with starred upper and lower borders, the U.S. Mint's 50 State Quarters® logo, and the words UNITED STATES MINT PROOF SET 2000.

Commentary: The popularity of the Mint's formerly lackluster silver Proof sets rose dramatically with the onset of the 50 State Quarters® Program in 1999, and this momentum carried through into 2000. This, combined with millennium Y2K mania, drove the number of pieces certified to very high levels.

Collector's Notebook – 2000
Leif Ericson silver dollar, reverse

142,900 of these fierce-looking silver dollars invaded coin collections in 2000. Honoring Leif Ericson's exploration of the New World, the coin was paired with a 10,000-kronor piece minted by the Republic of Iceland.

2,294,043 Ten-Piece Sets; 799,231 Five-Piece Sets

Denomination	PF-69 Ultra Cameo	
	Cert. Population	Value
Cent	3,376	
Nickel	3,434	
Dime	1,188	
Half Dollar	1,540	
Dollar	9,587	
New York Quarter	3,817	
North Carolina Quarter	4,029	
Rhode Island Quarter	3,555	
Vermont Quarter	3,539	
Kentucky Quarter	3,599	
Complete Clad Proof Set		$185

Original Price: $19.95 ten-piece set; $13.95 five-piece set

Uncertified Value: $150 ten-piece set; $60 five-piece set

Original Packaging: Two similar holders were required to house the ten coins, and they differed only in their inserts and the selection of coins included. Each holder consisted of a two-piece, transparent plastic casing with frosted borders. This held a blue fiberboard insert featuring a background graphic of the American flag and holed appropriately for the coins it contained. One holder housed the cent, nickel, dime, half dollar, and dollar, while the other contained the five statehood quarters for 2001. The two holders were stacked and slipped into a white cardboard box. This box was printed primarily in blue and featured a head shot of the Statue of Liberty, along with starred upper and lower borders, the U.S. Mint's 50 State Quarters® logo, and the words UNITED STATES MINT PROOF SET 2001.

The five-piece sets consisted solely of the statehood quarters in copper-nickel clad composition. The holder for this set was simply one of the two holders comprising the complete set described above. An eagle appears on the box cover in place of the Statue of Liberty.

Commentary: Sales of the regular ten-piece and five-piece Proof sets dropped off a bit in 2001. The popularity of the state quarters remained very high, but the added fuel of the Millennium was not present this year.

While the quality of Proof sets in recent decades has generally been of a consistently high level, some collectors observed that Proofs dated 2001 did not possess the depth of frosting seen in previous years. While deep cameo or ultra cameo Proofs certainly are not rare in an absolute sense, they do seem to be more elusive than usual.

A note of caution is in order regarding the net mintage figures of this and other Proof sets of recent vintage. Since the mid-1990s, the U.S. Mint has been slow in reporting sales, while its own annual reports may include incomplete or contradictory information.

While a discrepancy in the reporting of a few thousand Proof sets will have no impact on their rarity or value, an example of the challenges facing catalogers and researchers is illustrated by an announcement the Mint made in the spring of 2002. It seemingly found an unsold remainder of regular, nine- and ten-piece Proof sets dated 1999, 2000, and 2001, numbering approximately 150,000 of each. These were briefly offered at a package price of $94.95 for one group of three sets or just $74.95 per group when 100 or more were ordered. When it was discovered that the sets had suffered some loss of quality while in storage (most likely the cents were changing color), the offer quickly had to be rescinded.

2001-S SILVER PROOF SET

889,697 Complete Sets Possible

Denomination	PF-69 Ultra Cameo	
	Cert. Population	Value
Cent	Listed under 2001-S clad set	
Nickel	Listed under 2001-S clad set	
Dime	2,150	
Half Dollar	2,729	
Dollar	Listed under 2001-S clad set	
New York Quarter	5,830	
North Carolina Quarter	5,844	
Rhode Island Quarter	5,841	
Vermont Quarter	5,785	
Kentucky Quarter	5,880	
Complete Silver Proof Set		$250

Original Price: $31.95

Uncertified Value: $155

Original Packaging: Two holders were required to house the ten coins. Each holder consisted of a two-piece, transparent plastic casing with frosted borders. This held a red fiberboard insert labeled "Silver," featuring a background graphic of the American flag and holed appropriately for the coins it contained. One holder housed the cent, nickel, dime, half dollar, and dollar, while the other contained the five statehood quarters for 2001. The two holders were stacked and slipped into a white cardboard box. This box was printed primarily in red and featured a head view of the Statue of Liberty, along with starred upper and lower borders, the U.S. Mint's 50 State Quarters® logo, and the words UNITED STATES MINT PROOF SET 2001.

Commentary: Despite fairly high sales for this set, the popularity of the state quarters has driven the value of this recent set to an impressive level. As with the clad Proofs dated 2001, the depth of cameo contrast is a bit diminished on some of these Proofs, and this likely accounts for the higher value of certified coins.

Collector's Notebook – 2001
American Buffalo silver dollar, obverse

Even with its relatively high mintage of almost 275,000 Proofs, the 2001 Buffalo silver dollar sold out in two weeks. This is no surprise, given its subject matter: an homage to the classic and popular Indian Head/Buffalo nickel of 1913 to 1938.

2,277,720 Ten-Piece Sets; 761,600 Five-Piece Sets

Denomination	PF-69 Ultra Cameo	
	Cert. Population	Value
Cent	3,572	
Nickel	4,030	
Dime	1,924	
Half Dollar	2,277	
Dollar	5,209	
Tennessee Quarter	3,822	
Ohio Quarter	3,628	
Louisiana Quarter	3,766	
Indiana Quarter	3,743	
Mississippi Quarter	3,730	
Clad Proof Sets		$200

Original Price: $19.95 ten-piece set; $13.95 five-piece set

Uncertified Value: $50 ten-piece set; $30 five-piece set

Original Packaging: Two similar holders were required to house the ten coins, and they differed only in their inserts and the selection of coins included. Each holder consisted of a two-piece, transparent plastic casing with frosted borders. This held a blue fiberboard insert featuring a background graphic of the American flag and holed appropriately for the coins it contained. One holder housed the cent, nickel, dime, half dollar, and dollar, while the other contained the five statehood quarters for 2002. The two holders were stacked and slipped into a white cardboard box. This box was printed primarily in blue and featured a head view of the Statue of Liberty, along with starred upper and lower borders, the U.S. Mint's 50 State Quarters® logo, and the words UNITED STATES MINT PROOF SET 2002.

The five-piece sets consisted solely of the statehood quarters in copper-nickel clad composition. The holder for this set was simply one of the two holders comprising the complete set described above. An eagle appears on the box cover in place of the Statue of Liberty.

Commentary: Sales of the 2002-S regular Proof set were satisfying, and it has enjoyed only a modest advance in value from the issue price.

The quality of the coins was consistent with those of the previous year, with some collectors complaining that the depth of frosting was again less than ideal. It remains to be seen what effect the Mint's new technology of applying a frosted finish to dies via laser cutting will have. As of this writing, laser frosting has been applied to medals but not yet to coins.

Collector's Notebook – 2002
West Point silver dollar, obverse

Almost 1.5 million West Point cadets marched into coin collections in 2002: that's five cadets on each of 282,743 Proof West Point silver dollars. The coins were struck to commemorate the military academy's 200th year of service.

2002-S SILVER PROOF SET

888,826 Complete Sets Possible

Denomination	PF-69 Ultra Cameo	
	Cert. Population	Value
Cent	Listed under 2002-S clad set	
Nickel	Listed under 2002-S clad set	
Dime	2,031	
Half Dollar	2,831	
Dollar	Listed under 2002-S clad set	
Tennessee Quarter	5,180	
Ohio Quarter	5,194	
Louisiana Quarter	5,020	
Indiana Quarter	5,155	
Mississippi Quarter	5,235	
Complete Silver Proof Set		$300

Original Price: $31.95

Uncertified Value: $80

Original Packaging: Two holders were required to house the ten coins. Each holder consisted of a two-piece, transparent plastic casing with frosted borders. This held a red fiberboard insert labeled "Silver," featuring a background graphic of the American flag and holed appropriately for the coins it contained. One holder housed the cent, nickel, dime, half dollar, and dollar, while the other contained the five statehood quarters for 2002. The two holders were stacked and slipped into a white cardboard box. This box was printed primarily in red and featured a head view of the Statue of Liberty, along with starred upper and lower borders, the U.S. Mint's 50 State Quarters® logo, and the words UNITED STATES MINT SILVER PROOF SET 2002.

Commentary: The popularity of the silver Proof set remained high in 2002. This is likely to continue through the projected end of the 50 State Quarters® Program in 2008, but what the Mint will do to entice buyers after that time is unknown.

Collector's Notebook – 2002
West Point silver dollar, reverse

Collectors who seek a Proof 2002 West Point silver dollar for their collections are advised to inspect the helmet on the reverse. With its smooth, open field at the center of the design, it can easily attract high-visibility blemishes.

2003-S CLAD PROOF SET

2,237,032 Ten-Piece Sets; 1,235,832 Five-Piece Sets

Denomination	PF-69 Ultra Cameo	
	Cert. Population	Value
Cent	7,618	
Nickel	7,808	
Dime	3,510	
Half Dollar	3,826	
Dollar	8,133	
Illinois Quarter	6,099	
Alabama Quarter	6,016	
Maine Quarter	6,220	
Missouri Quarter	5,835	
Arkansas Quarter	5,920	
Complete Clad Proof Set		$200

Original Price: $19.95 ten-piece set; $13.95 five-piece set

Uncertified Value: $40 ten-piece set; $29 five-piece set

Original Packaging: Two similar holders were required to house the ten coins, and they differed only in their inserts and the selection of coins included. Each holder consisted of a two-piece, transparent plastic casing with frosted borders. This held a blue fiberboard insert featuring a background graphic of the American flag and holed appropriately for the coins it contained. One holder housed the cent, nickel, dime, half dollar, and dollar, while the other contained the five statehood quarters for 2003. The two holders were stacked and slipped into a white cardboard box. This box was printed primarily in blue and featured a head view of the famous Statue of Liberty, along with starred upper and lower borders, the U.S. Mint's 50 State Quarters® logo, and the words UNITED STATES MINT PROOF SET 2003.

The five-piece sets consisted solely of the statehood quarters in copper-nickel clad composition. The holder for this set was simply one of the two holders comprising the complete set described above. An eagle appears on the box cover in place of the Statue of Liberty.

Commentary: This year's sets seem to be a repeat of 2002. Both collector interest and quality are high, but not to the same degree as for earlier entries in the 50 State Quarters® Program.

One clear observation can be made with respect to Proof coins of recent years. The Mint's goal of lowering the relief of the dies and sharpening their details has been fully achieved. It seems that neither operation can be taken much further, and the coins being minted today look very much as they did ten years ago, the sole exception being the ongoing changes to the quarter. Technical perfection seems to have triumphed over artistry, but this is of little consequence to those seeking Proofs for that very perfection.

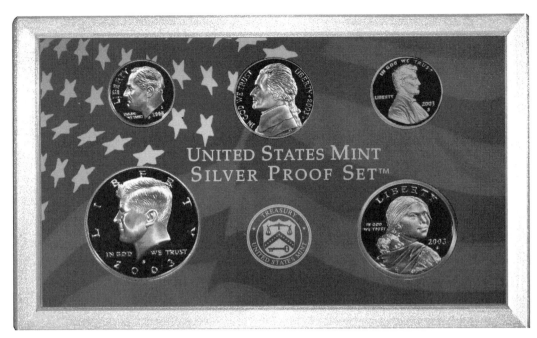

1,113,349 Complete Sets Possible

Denomination	PF-69 Ultra Cameo	
	Cert. Population	Value
Cent	Listed under 2003-S clad set	
Nickel	Listed under 2003-S clad set	
Dime	3,909	
Half Dollar	4,185	
Dollar	Listed under 2003-S clad set	
Illinois Quarter	5,816	
Alabama Quarter	5,689	
Maine Quarter	5,666	
Missouri Quarter	5,742	
Arkansas Quarter	5,755	
Complete Silver Proof Set		$300

Original Price: $31.95

Uncertified Value: $40

Original Packaging: Two holders were required to house the ten coins. Each holder consisted of a two-piece, transparent plastic casing with frosted borders. This held a red fiberboard insert labeled "Silver", featuring a background graphic of the American flag and holed appropriately for the coins it contained. One holder housed the cent, nickel, dime, half dollar, and dollar, while the other contained the five statehood quarters for 2003. The two holders were stacked and slipped into a white cardboard box. This box was printed primarily in red and featured a head view of the famous Statue of Liberty, along with starred upper and lower borders, the U.S. Mint's 50 State Quarters® logo, and the words UNITED STATES MINT SILVER PROOF SET 2003.

Commentary: Sales of this set were up considerably from previous years, this being the first instance that the total topped one million sets. This seems to have had a dampening effect on the secondary market for these sets, with values hovering around issue price. This may prove to be a temporary phenomenon, as prices typically rise over the long term.

Collector's Notebook – 2003
First Flight silver dollar, reverse

In 1903 the Wright brothers made their first successful powered flight, at Kill Devil Hill, North Carolina. This 2003 commemorative silver dollar honored their achievement. Collectors will find perfect PF-70 examples to be as elusive as vintage biplanes.

1,414,062 Eleven-Piece Sets; 783,459 Five-Piece Sets

(Both of the above figures are incomplete and will likely rise.)

Denomination	PF-69 Ultra Cameo	
	Population	Value
Cent	2,644	
Nickel (Peace)	4,317	
Nickel (Keelboat)	4,363	
Dime	1,391	
Half Dollar	2,006	
Dollar	4,089	
Michigan Quarter	3,623	
Florida Quarter	3,697	
Texas Quarter	3,605	
Iowa Quarter	3,532	
Wisconsin Quarter	3,611	
Complete Clad Proof Set		$200

Original Price: $22.95 ten-piece set; $15.95 five-piece set

Uncertified Value: $75 eleven-piece set; $32 five-piece set

Original Packaging: Two similar holders were required to house the eleven coins, and they differed only in their inserts and the selection of coins included. Each holder consisted of a two-piece, transparent plastic casing with frosted borders. This held a blue fiberboard insert featuring a background graphic of the American flag and holed appropriately for the coins it contained. One holder housed the cent, two nickels, dime, half dollar, and dollar, while the other contained the five statehood quarters for 2004. The two holders were stacked and slipped into a white cardboard box. This box was printed primarily in blue and featured a head view of the famous Statue of Liberty, along with starred upper and lower borders, the U.S. Mint's 50 State Quarters® logo, and the words UNITED STATES MINT PROOF SET 2004.

The five-piece sets consisted solely of the statehood quarters in copper-nickel clad composition. The holder for this set was simply one of the two holders comprising the complete set described above. An eagle appears on the box cover in place of the Statue of Liberty.

Commentary: The quality of the 2004-S clad Proof sets seems to be satisfactory, though there are still some complaints that the desired degree of frosting on the coins' devices is not always maintained.

The big news for 2004 was the inclusion of two nickels in place of the usual single entry. While the obverse of this coin type retained the familiar bust of Thomas Jefferson, two distinctive reverses were employed in celebration of the Louisiana Purchase and Lewis and Clark bicentennials, respectively.

The first of the new nickels featured on its reverse an adaptation of the reverse from an Indian Peace medal of the type distributed to American Indian chiefs during and for many years after the administration of President Jefferson. It shows a pair of clasped hands, one wrist bearing a military cuff and the other a bracelet. The implication is that these hands belong to a U. S. Army officer and a Native American engaged in a bond of peace and friendship. Above the hands are a crossed tomahawk and peace pipe, the legend LOUISIANA PURCHASE, and the date of its signing, 1803.

The second of the two nickels issued for circulation (and included in the Proof sets for 2004) depicts members of the Lewis and Clark Voyage of Discovery expedition embarked in a keelboat. These two coins are the first in the Westward Journey Nickel Series™. Other designs for 2005 include the Bison reverse and the Pacific Ocean reverse.

2004-S SILVER PROOF SET

655,766 Eleven-Piece Sets; 601,671 Five-Piece Sets

(These figures will likely rise as a final accounting is made.)

| Denomination | PF-69 Ultra Cameo | |
	Population	Value
Cent	Listed under 2004-S clad set	
Nickel	Listed under 2004-S clad set	
Dime	1,427	
Half Dollar	1,696	
Dollar	Listed under 2004-S clad set	
Michigan Quarter	5,279	
Florida Quarter	5,319	
Texas Quarter	5,478	
Iowa Quarter	5,479	
Wisconsin Quarter	5,513	
Complete Silver Proof Set		$300

Original Price: $37.95 eleven-piece set: $23.95 five-piece set

Uncertified Value: $45 eleven-piece set; $38 five-piece set

Original Packaging: Two holders were required to house the eleven coins. Each holder consisted of a two-piece, transparent plastic casing with frosted borders. This held a red fiberboard insert labeled "Silver," featuring a background graphic of the American flag and holed appropriately for the coins it contained. One holder housed the cent, two nickels, dime, half dollar, and dollar, while the other contained the five statehood quarters for 2004. The two holders were stacked and slipped into a white cardboard box. This box was printed primarily in red and featured a head view of the famous Statue of Liberty, along with starred upper and lower borders, the U.S. Mint's 50 State Quarters® logo, and the words UNITED STATES MINT SILVER PROOF SET 2004.

The five-piece sets consisted solely of the statehood quarters in 90% silver composition. The holder for this set was simply one of the two holders comprising the complete set described above. An eagle appears on the box cover in place of the Statue of Liberty.

Commentary: As is usually the case with the U.S. Mint's silver proofs, the quality of these coins is outstanding. Ultra cameo contrast is the norm.

In addition to featuring two nickels in place of the usual single coin, the U. S. Mint introduced a new sales option for the first time this year. Five-piece Proof sets of the copper-nickel clad statehood quarters had been available since the onset of the 50 State Quarters® Program in 1999, but now a corresponding set of silver quarters was offered at $23.95. The price of the eleven-piece set was raised six dollars due to inclusion of a second nickel and the adoption of a revised insert to hold it.

Final mintage quantities not available at press time

Original Price: $22.95 eleven-piece set; $15.95 five-piece set

Uncertified Value: $22.95 eleven-piece set; $15.95 five-piece set

Original Packaging: Two similar holders house the eleven coins, differing only in their inserts and the selection of coins included. Each holder consists of a two-piece transparent plastic casing with frosted borders. This holds a blue fiberboard insert (featuring a background graphic of the American flag), holed appropriately for its coins. One holder houses the cent, two nickels, dime, half dollar, and dollar, while the other contains the five statehood quarters for 2005. The two holders are stacked and packaged into a white cardboard box printed primarily in blue and featuring a head view of the Statue of Liberty, along with starred upper and lower borders, the U.S. Mint's 50 State Quarters® logo, and the words UNITED STATES MINT PROOF SET 2005.

The five-piece sets consist solely of the statehood quarters in copper-nickel clad composition. The holder for this set is simply one of the two holders comprising the complete set described above. An eagle appears on the box cover in place of the Statue of Liberty.

Commentary: The 11-piece 2005-S Proof set contains the statehood quarters for California, Minnesota, Oregon, Kansas, and West Virginia.

As with the 2004 sets, the quality of the 2005-S clad Proof sets seems to be satisfactory, though some complaints are heard regarding the frosting. As of this writing the sets remain available from the U. S. Mint; a final determination of their overall quality is still pending.

As in 2004, the 2005 proof set includes two nickels in place of the usual single entry. These coins are likewise part of the U. S. Mint's Westward Journey Nickel Series™. The familiar Houdon bust of Thomas Jefferson is depicted again, but in a new interpretation by Joe Fitzgerald. Recruited as part of the Mint's Artistic Infusion Program, Fitzgerald chose to show America's third president in profile, but with a slight turn toward the viewer. In a novel twist, the legend LIBERTY is reproduced in Jefferson's own handwriting. The reverse of this feature portrays a bison standing upon a mound, reminiscent of James Earle Fraser's nickel design of 1913. Though described by the Mint in its literature with the zoologically correct term "bison," it seems likely that collectors will ultimately call this new coin a "buffalo nickel," harkening back to the popular Fraser design still known by that name. In an interesting coincidence, the Kansas statehood quarter issued this year bears a similar reverse, marking the only instance that the U. S. Mint has struck two different bison coins in a single year.

The second issue for 2005 is the fourth and final entry in the Westward Journey series. Appearing early in the year as part of the Proof sets, it was not released to circulation until midyear. Combined with the Fitzgerald portrait of Jefferson is a distinctive reverse depicting the Pacific Ocean as it must have looked to Lewis and Clark as they stood near the mouth of the Columbia River. A journal entry by William Clark from November 7, 1805 reads (with some liberty taken in correcting his spelling), "Ocean in view! O! The joy!" This memorable quote is reproduced on the reverse of the nickel.

2005-S Silver Proof Set: The silver Proof coin sets are not available for study as of press time. Their uncertified value has not risen above their original price of $37.95 for the eleven-piece set and $23.95 for the five-piece set.

Looking Forward

The U. S. Mint's offerings of Proof sets have come a long way since 1936. In addition to providing numerous packaging and price options to satisfy every collector, the quality of the Mint's Proof coins has become virtually unimprovable. Whether one chooses to preserve them in their original packaging, place them in coin albums, or have them graded and encapsulated, the end result will be a collection that is beautiful to display and of lasting historic and sentimental value.

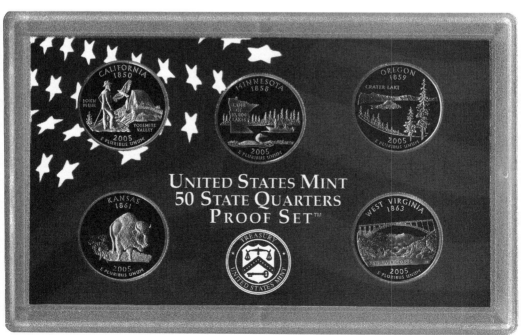

20TH-CENTURY PROOF COIN
AUCTION RECORDS, BY TYPE

This chart (reflecting auction data available through late 2004) illustrates the highest prices realized at auction for the coins you'll find in your modern Proof sets. Some coin series, especially those currently circulating, have seen no significant auction activity, and are not listed.

Type and Date: The coins series, the date of the particular coin auctioned, and any variety details.
Grade: The grade assigned by the service that slabbed the coin.
Price: The price realized at auction (typically including a 15% buyer's fee).
Sale: The name of the auction sale, and its month and year.

SMALL CENTS

TYPE and DATE	GRADE	PRICE	SALE
Lincoln, Wheat Ears, 1910	PCGS PR-67RD	$36,800	Mid-Winter ANA, March 2003
Lincoln, Memorial, 1963	PCGS PR-70DC	$40,250	FUN Signature #336, Jan 2004

NICKEL FIVE-CENT PIECES

TYPE and DATE	GRADE	PRICE	SALE
Indian Head, 1915	NGC PR-69	$52,900	CSNS, May 2003
Jefferson, Monticello, 1952	NGC PR-69UCAM	$8,913	FUN Signature #336, Jan 2004
Jefferson, Wartime, 1942-P	PCGS PR-66CAM	$2,818	ANA Signature #352, Aug 2004

DIMES

TYPE and DATE	GRADE	PRICE	SALE
Winged Liberty, 1939	NGC PR-69	$14,375	Long Beach, Feb 2003
Roosevelt, Silver, 1951	NGC PR-68DC	$6,325	ANA Signature #352, Aug 2004
Roosevelt, Clad, 1968 No S	PCGS PR-67	$5,635	Bristol, March 2001

QUARTER DOLLARS

TYPE and DATE	GRADE	PRICE	SALE
Washington, Silver, 1942	NGC PR-69 Star	$14,950	Pre-FUN, Jan 2004

HALF DOLLARS

TYPE and DATE	GRADE	PRICE	SALE
Liberty Walking, 1936	PCGS PR-68	$74,750	CSNS, May 2004
Franklin, 1953	PCGS PR-67DC	$14,375	Long Beach, Sept 2002

BIBLIOGRAPHY

Gale, Bill, and Ronald Guth. *United States Proof Sets and Mint Sets 1936–2002*. Edina, MN: New York Mint, Ltd., 2002.

Tomaska, Rick Jerry. *Cameo and Brilliant Proof Coinage of the 1950 to 1970 Era*. Encinitas, CA: R&I Publications, 1991.

Yeoman, R. S. (Kenneth Bressett, editor). *A Guide Book of United States Coins*. Atlanta, GA: Whitman Publishing, LLC, published annually.

Surviving Proof coins of 1936 vary in their quality today. Many have weathered the years poorly, showing streaks, toning, and other signs of age. Still, they include some of the most beautiful and enduring of all United States coin designs.

Lincoln Wheat Ears Cent

Proof Lincoln wheat ears cents of the 1936 to 1942 and 1950 to 1958 eras appear mostly with dies polished overall. Some later issues have frosted ("cameo") portraits.

Indian Head/Buffalo Nickel

Proof Indian Head nickels of 1936 are found with a satiny finish and also with a mirror finish in the fields. Proofs of 1937 have a mirror surface. The design elements of the 1936 and 1937 mirror Proofs are lightly polished in the die (not frosty or matte).

Winged Liberty/"Mercury" Dime

Proofs of the Winged Liberty dime were struck only from 1936 to 1942, with later dates having higher mintages. They were struck from completely polished dies (including the portrait).

Washington Quarter Dollar

Proofs of the silver Washington quarter dollar are plentiful and usually very attractive. The mintage numbers of vintage coins (of 1936 to 1942) increase by date, from a low of 3,837 to a high of 21,123. Washington quarter Proofs were also stuck in silver from 1950 to 1964.

Liberty Walking Half Dollar

Proof half dollars were minted from 1936 through 1942. They are usually fairly well struck. Most Proofs of 1941 were coined from dies polished so excessively that the designer's initials (AW for Adolph Weinman) are no longer visible.

PROOF COIN PACKAGING

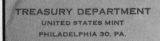

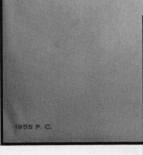

Proof Coins of 1955

If you had placed your order for a Proof set early in 1955, your coins would have been delivered in individual envelopes stapled together and wrapped in tissue paper for protection, then sealed inside a small cardboard box with postal tape (rubber-stamped 1955 UNITED STATES PROOF COINS).

Starting midway through the year, the Mint adopted a single "pliofilm" envelope with individually sealed compartments. This flexible holder would be inserted, along with two pieces of stiff cardstock, into a manila envelope.

Bicentennial Packaging

The 1976-S Bicentennial Silver Set consisted of three coins (the quarter dollar, half dollar, and dollar), each encased in its own acrylic capsule. These were displayed in an attractive wallet-like case, hinged to allow both sides of the coins to be viewed.

The silver Bicentennial coins, double-dated 1776–1976, each saw a mintage of approximately four million pieces in Proof. Their designs were submitted to the Treasury after it announced an open contest in October 1973. Dennis R. Williams designed the dollar reverse, featuring the Liberty Bell superimposed over the moon; Seth G. Huntington designed the half dollar's rendition of Independence Hall in Philadelphia; and Jack L. Ahr designed the quarter dollar's depiction of a colonial drummer with a victory torch and stars.

Sooner or later your Proof Coins may show evidence of oxidation (tarnish or discoloration). We have chosen materials and methods which we hope will delay this possibility, but we cannot assume responsibility for oxidation.

Please do not ask us to make exchanges or adjustments.

Your U.S. Proof Coins have been carefully inspected before release!

If there should appear—what may seem to you—a defect or scratch on a coin—it is, no doubt, a crease in the polyethylene-coated mylar. We tell you this to save us both unnecessary correspondence.

Thank you!

(Mrs.) RAE V. BIESTER,
Superintendent.

U.S. GOVERNMENT PRINTING OFFICE : 1969—O-562454

Your U.S. Proof Coins have been carefully inspected, and then sealed in a transparent envelope. This package was designed to prevent or delay tarnishing and discoloration. Nevertheless, sooner or later tarnishing may occur. Care in handling and storing will help to prolong the newly-minted luster of the coins; heat and direct sunlight are especially harmful.

Please do not ask us to make exchanges or adjustments.

If there should appear—what may seem to you—a defect or scratch on a coin—it is, no doubt, a crease in the packaging material. We tell you this to save us both unnecessary correspondence.

Superintendent,
U.S. Mint,
Philadelphia, Pa.

¶ GPO 1962 OF—421766

Your U.S. Proof Coins—

have been carefully inspected before release!

If there should appear—what may seem to you—a defect or a scratch on a coin—it is no doubt a crease in the polyethylene-coated cellophane in which they are encased.

We tell you this to save us both unnecessary correspondence. THANK YOU!

RAE V. BIESTER,
Superintendent.

GPO : 1969—O-505424

YOUR U.S. PROOF COINS
have been carefully inspected before release!

If there should appear – what may seem to you – a defect or a scratch on a coin, – it is no doubt a crease in the polyethylene-coated cellophane in which they are encased.

We tell you this to save us both unnecessary correspondence. THANK YOU!

Rae V. Biester
Superintendent

Bureau of the Mint, Treasury Department, Washington, D. C. 20220

Dear Friend:

These coins, which constitute our first issue of United States Special Mint Sets, were struck at the U. S. Assay Office at San Francisco, California. In addition to the 1965 dated nickel and cent pieces, the set contains three new clad coins authorized by the Coinage Act of 1965.

Special Mint Sets are made from specially prepared and polished blanks and struck on high tonnage presses with polished dies. We have endeavored to minimize scratches and discoloration. It is possible that tarnishing and discoloration may occur, particularly if removed from the packages, and if exposed to heat or direct sunlight. We cannot undertake to make exchanges.

Your name has been added to the mailing list kept by the United States Assay Office at San Francisco and you will be sent order blanks for such new issues as may be offered for sale.

We hope these coins will be pleasing to you, and that we may have the privilege, again, of serving you.

DIRECTOR OF THE MINT

The United States Mint certifies that these proof versions of current United States circulating coinage were produced and packaged at the United States Mint, San Francisco, California. Each coin bears the mint mark "S" designation of that facility.

United States proof coins are produced from carefully selected planchets, or blanks, that have been burnished to a high luster. The polished blanks, which are carefully handled to minimize scratches and abrasions, are struck on specially adapted coining presses. Each coin is struck at least twice to bring forth the most minute detail with remarkable clarity.

The surfaces of the coinage dies for striking proof coins are meticulously processed to create a frosted appearance of the image on the die. The background surface is polished and buffed to a mirror-like finish. The dies are also buffed during the striking process.

The finished coin with its frosted cameo image on a mirror-like field is carefully inspected--with gloved hands to protect its surface--before being assembled into sets. The proof coins are then placed into transparent presentation cases.

Proof coins, referred to as "Master Coins" in the early days of the Mint, were originally produced to "prove the correctness of the dies." These first pieces, struck with extra care and bearing a high polish, were reserved for the Mint's Cabinet of Coins Collection and sometimes used for special presentations. They were first offered for sale to the public in approximately 1858 and are produced under the authority of Section 5111 (a)(3), Title 31 of the United States Code.

Proof coins are a supplemental program of the United States Mint, produced at no net cost to the government, with profits deposited to the General Fund of the Treasury of the United States.

Eugene H. Essner
Eugene H. Essner
Deputy Director of the Mint

1986 Proof Coin Set
Specifications

Denomination	Cent	Nickel	Dime	Quarter	Half Dollar
Obverse	Lincoln	Jefferson	Roosevelt	Washington	Kennedy
Designed by	V.D. Brenner	Felix Schlag	John R. Sinnock	John Flanagan	Gilroy Roberts
Reverse	Lincoln Memorial	Monticello	Torch, Olive Branch, Oak Branch	Heraldic Eagle	Heraldic Eagle
Designed by	Frank Gasparro	Felix Schlag	John R. Sinnock	John Flanagan	Frank Gasparro
Composition	Copper-plated Zinc 2.6% Cu Balance Zn	Cupro-Nickel 25% Ni Balance Cu	Cupro-Nickel Clad 8.33% Ni Balance Cu	Cupro-Nickel Clad 8.33% Ni Balance Cu	Cupro-Nickel Clad 8.33% Ni Balance Cu
Standard Weight	2.500 g	5.000 g	2.268 g	5.670 g	11.340 g
Standard Diameter	0.750 in. 19.05 mm	0.835 in. 21.21 mm	0.705 in. 17.91 mm	0.955 in. 24.26 mm	1.205 in. 30.61 mm
Edge					

CERTIFICATE OF AUTHENTICITY

The United States Mint certifies that these proof versions of current United States circulating coinage were produced and packaged at the United States Mint, San Francisco, California. Each coin bears the mintmark "S" designation of this facility.

United States proof coins are produced from carefully selected planchets, or blanks, that have been burnished to a high luster. The polished blanks, which are carefully handled to minimize scratches and abrasions, are struck on specially adapted coining presses. Each coin is struck at least twice to bring forth the most minute detail with remarkable clarity.

The surfaces of the coinage dies for striking proof coins are meticulously processed to create a frosted appearance of the image on the die. The background surface is polished and buffed to a mirror-like finish. The dies are also buffed during the striking process.

The finished coin with its frosted cameo image on a mirror-like field is carefully inspected—with gloved hands to protect its surface—before being assembled into sets. The proof coins are then placed into transparent presentation cases.

Proof coins, referred to as "Master Coins" in the early days of the Mint, were originally produced to "prove the correctness of the dies." These first pieces, struck with extra care and bearing a high polish, were reserved for the Mint's Cabinet of Coins Collection and sometimes used for special presentations. They were first offered for sale to the public in approximately 1858 and are produced under the authority of Section 5111 (a)(3), Title 31 of the United States Code.

Proof coins are a supplemental program of the United States Mint, produced at no net cost to the government, with profits deposited to the General Fund of the Treasury of the United States.

Donna J. Pope
Director of the Mint

Proof Set Inserts of Yesteryear

Over the years, various inserts have been included with the U.S. Mint's Proof sets. Bearing the facsimile signatures of Mint directors, superintendents, and other officers, these cards offer proof of authenticity, friendly advice, instructions, coin specifications, helpful information, and notes of thanks.